The
Encyclopedia
of
Astrology

The Encyclopedia of Astrology

Sandra Shulman

Hamlyn

London · New York · Sydney · Toronto

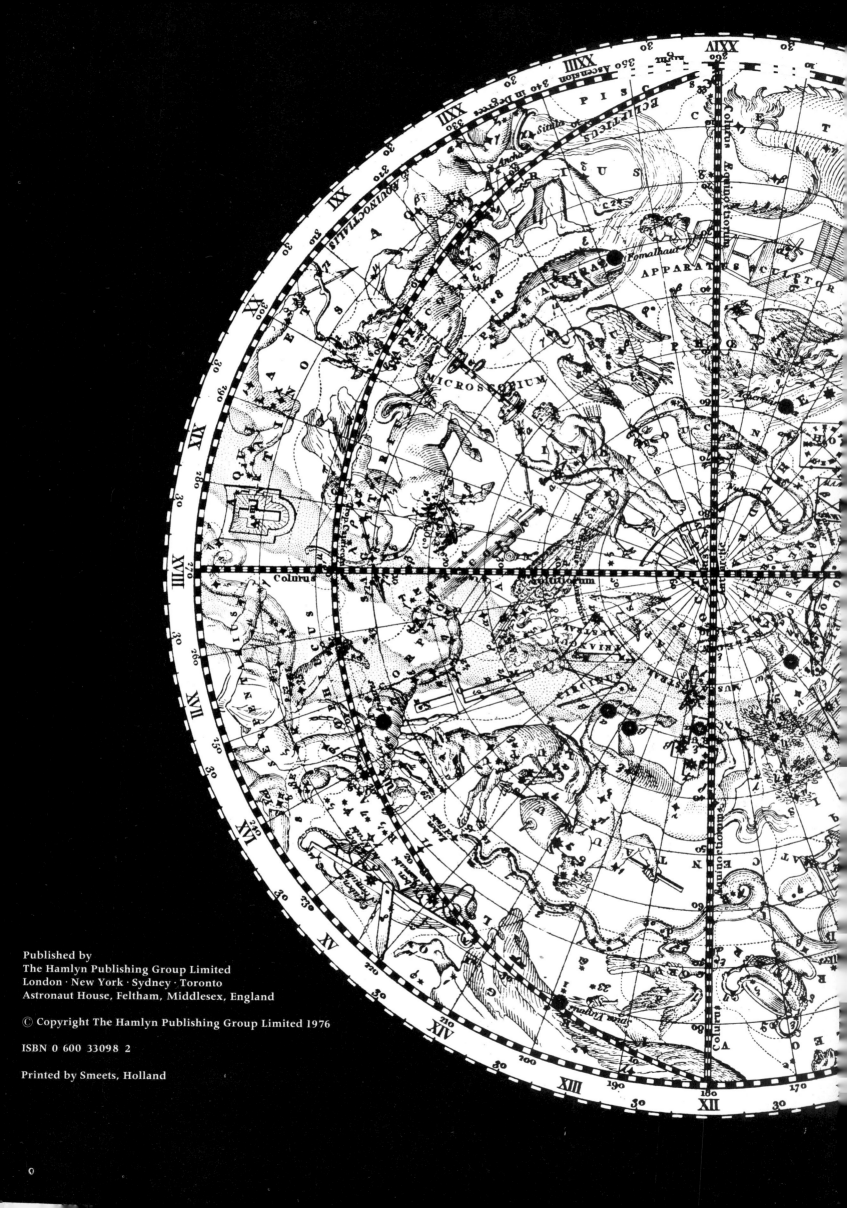

Published by
The Hamlyn Publishing Group Limited
London · New York · Sydney · Toronto
Astronaut House, Feltham, Middlesex, England

© Copyright The Hamlyn Publishing Group Limited 1976

ISBN 0 600 33098 2

Printed by Smeets, Holland

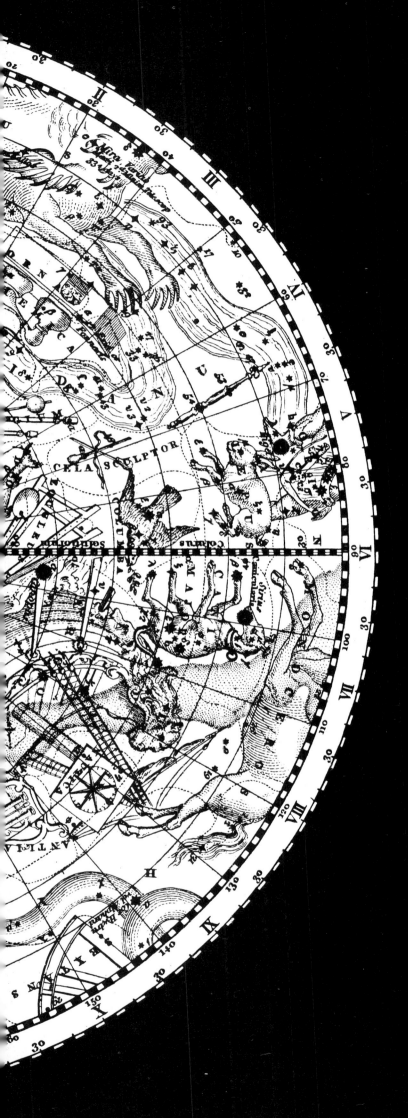

Contents

Endpaper:
Gaseous nebula in Serpens, photographed by a
200-inch telescope.

Title page:
The Orlog or astronomical clock on the tower of
the old Town Hall, Prague.

Introduction

Opposite page:
The simple homilies and rough woodcuts of the ordinary calendar gave the farmer and craftsman their seasonal information. Great nobles read the same sort of lore in magnificently illuminated manuscripts, decorated with the signs of the zodiac. December. Page from 'Les très riches heures du Duc de Berry'. Fifteenth-century French manuscript. Musée Condé, Chantilly.

Twentieth-century man would claim to be very different from his ancestors of 5000 or more years ago. After all, he has been to the moon and back, and sent rockets far beyond. Yet, peel away that thin veneer of sophistication, information and knowledge which most of us have acquired, and we discover just how akin is our secret mind to that of people who would be completely bewildered by the world we now inhabit. Like them we feel the mystery of the universe and seek some sort of unity with it.

Despite present-day knowledge and technology – so unlike anything dreamed of by those ancients – we share certain of their beliefs, for there are some which are fundamental to the human condition. While the rational and the scientific attack astrology many people all over the world still believe – or want to believe – that in some mysterious way their lives are governed by the movements of the stars, no matter what is established to the contrary. This does not prove anything about astrology, but it does show that if it had simply been another gimcrack craze with no more substance than a fantasy, it would by now have passed into the realms of quaint superstition and folklore. The persistence of the concept in the face of much daunting evidence and argument demonstrates how deep and archetypal it is. The fact that more

and more people are drawn to examine and countenance a star-ruled fate – even at the apparently superficial level of buying some astrological almanac at a station bookstall – relates to a primitive need as basic as love, fighting, or food.

Conquest, trade, and nomadic migrations account for the dissemination and expansion of ideas, but certain beliefs do arise independently in totally unconnected parts of the world, because man is everywhere prey to the same fundamental fears and longings.

Whatever the latitude or longitude the sky is common to all. We may therefore assume that earliest man, while he struggled for survival and long before he left posterity any written records or erected great patterns of stones to show he had marked the movements of the greater luminaries, observed the heavens, wondered at the sun, moon, and stars, feared the darkness of eclipses, and tried to relate these celestial phenomena to events nearer home. Herdsmen, fishermen, and primitive farmers must have all looked to these signs to find if they were propitious for the tasks needing to be tackled. Closer to the hearth women must have measured the menstrual cycle and the span of pregnancy against the visiting moon.

Great or lowly, man has always desired to believe that his own and his children's lives meant more than a brief period of troubled and painful toil curtailed by death. Most of us are arrogant or hopeful enough to insist that our individual fates cannot be mere accidents: all our striving would seem utterly futile if there were no reason for living.

Man has ever looked heavenwards for a clue to the meaning of existence, holding to the idea of 'as above so below'. Since he is a part – however insignificant – of a systematically ordered world, there must be some relationship between himself and the cosmos. Thus, the movements of the celestial bodies should affect what takes place on earth. If these signs could be read properly, the meaning of the universe might be understood, and the future revealed and provided for.

Even at the most prosaic level of 'shall I eat tomorrow?' (and for our earliest ancestors hunting for food was a major preoccupation) man has tried to find out about the future. Seeing himself at the mercy of forces beyond his control and understanding, he has been unwilling to accept the entire responsibility for his

Man the ever-curious peering out of the universe at the mechanism which was then thought to rule the planets. Sixteenth-century German woodcut.

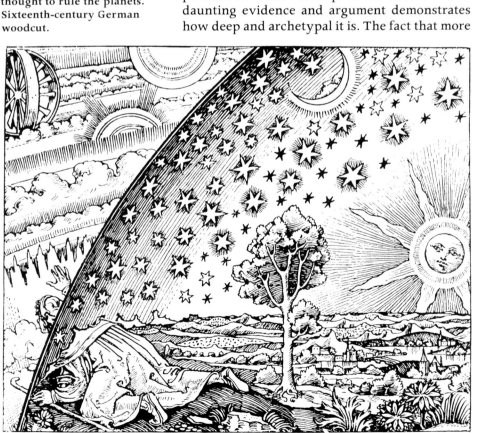

10

11

'The Resurrection' by Fra Angelico. Easter falls at the spring equinox, a time noted and celebrated among the ancients long before the advent of Christianity. Museo di San Marco, Florence.

own and the world's fate, and so he has created gods to aid him, to placate and to blame, and rituals by which to worship and appease them. He gave these gods guardianship of the mysteries of heaven and earth, and appointed priests or magicians to act as intermediaries and interpret whatever signs the gods sent. Man located his basic terrors and pleasures in the natures of these gods, and although they possessed supernatural powers he also endowed them with human characteristics and frailities. Thus they were not too lofty to squabble, have moods, or be angry.

Nowadays, astrology is a maligned and battered lady of dubious reputation and ancient antecedents. Popularity has debased and trivialized this once royal art into an entertainment. Yet, astrology was born about the same time as religion and astronomy. Indeed, the study of the stars had an important place in most religions, and must have been among man's earliest scientific experiments, together with making fire or sowing seed. Moreover, medicine is one of astrology's close relatives.

Before we try to define astrology, let us consider what we all know about it. Nearly everyone–no matter how indifferent or scathing–knows his birth sign. We also employ the conventionally accepted characteristics of the heavenly bodies, inherited from ancient times, to describe anything from people to music. So we have 'jovial', 'sunny', 'mercurial'. ' saturnine', and 'martial', and when we speak of someone 'mooning' around this is because the moon was at one time held to govern dreams. In many languages the names of the days of the week

Henry Cornelius Agrippa—
court physician in sixteenth-
century France whose research
into astrology led him to write:
'At length I learned that
wholly and altogether it was
based upon no other
foundation but upon mere
trifles, and feignings of
imaginations'. Sixteenth-
century engraving by Thevet.

One of the celestial maps from
Andreas Cellarius' 'Atlas
Coelestis seu Harmonia
Macrocosmica' (1661).
Baynton-Williams Gallery,
Belgravia, London.

STELLATI
ANI HÆ
RIUM PRIUS.

15

Christmas falls at the winter solstice when the ancients celebrated the returning of the sun, and Easter coincides with the spring equinox when the land has shed its dour winter overcoat. Astronomers—who cannot be regarded as friends of astrology—use astrologers' ideograms for the planets and constellations, and so their charts bear some resemblance to the much-maligned horoscope. As we explore the subject we shall see that these are no clever coincidences, but the result of long-established beliefs which no amount of sweet reason can quite replace.

The conflicting statements made about it during the course of history by various authorities show that there is no simple answer to the nature of astrology. Nor is it made any clearer by the mass of books written on the subject: writings that range from those ubiquitous astrological booklets dealing with individual birth signs, through learned, repetitive and often boring tomes, to the ancient cuneiform script of the Babylonians.

At the most popular level astrology has degenerated into a machine giving you a ticket which tells your fortune along with your weight, or the daily newspaper horoscope shared by countless others. Such columns and astrological almanacs have millions of enthusiastic readers throughout the world. One English Sunday newspaper receives about 100,000 letters yearly addressed to its astrologer. At the more esoteric level it has become so swathed in obscurity as to give its critics an ample supply of ammunition with which to bombard unproven 'facts'.

demonstrate how once they were thought to be ruled by particular deities, who had their abodes in the sky.

Our ideas on the measurement of time have much to do with astrological ritual. There are twelve months, and twelve signs of the zodiac. A month is the period of time between two moons. Weeks are quarters of a month, and the moon has four quarters. The day is divided into twenty-four hours, which is two sets of the zodiac. Even the respectable dates on our calendar once had astrological significance:

Astronomers contemplating the sky in the daytime and at night. Sixteenth-century engraving.

Our space-age astrology, with its centuries of accumulated lore, arguments, and even mis-calculations, is a repository of beliefs, teachings and wisdom of long ago. Ideas and practices have been grafted on to one other until it is difficult to find the true beginnings. To discover the deepest roots of astrology we need the help of those painstaking time detectives – the archaeologists and the students of ancient languages.

The following chapters are an attempt to throw some light on the subject without taking sides. Whether you regard astrology with a mixture of amusement and doubt, or avidly believe your fate is controlled by the stars, in seeking out the origins and development of this 'chimera' you will be adding to your own store of knowledge about the human race.

Our journey of exploration should start at the very beginning . . . or as near as we can get to it. As we work our way forward to our own times the signs along the route may acquire greater dimension, and their meanings assume a fresh significance.

In many languages the days of the week are named after gods who had their abode in particular planets. In these woodcuts from a late fifteenth/ early sixteenth-century edition of 'The Shepheards Kalendar', an English translation of 'Icy est le Compost', the days are shown in order of the supposed distance of the planets from the earth. Royal Astronomical Society, London.

Saturne .	Jupiter .	Mars	Sol .	Uenus
Saturday	Thursday.	Tuesday.	Sunday.	Friday.

A Vocabulary of Astrology

On any journey through a foreign land it is sensible to have maps, guide books, and a simple phrasebook. Travelling in the maze of information about astrology may be less bewildering if you are first familiar with a number of terms which will occur from time to time. Here are some of the main ones. Explanations of how they arose will appear later in the book.

There are many different types of astrology. **Natural**–now incorporated into astronomy, for it predicts the movements of the heavenly bodies.

Judicial–predicts how these motions will affect life on earth, and is divided as follows:

Mundane–dealing only with the fortunes of a nation and its ruler as head of the state. Also used to foretell world disasters.

Genethliacal–the art of drawing and reading an individual's horoscope: the most popular kind of astrology.

Horary–reading the horoscope for the moment in order to answer particular questions. No longer favoured by astrologers but once very popular.

Medical–concerned with the mineral salts of the body which are related to the signs of the zodiac. The movements of the planets are read to deduce what salts the body lacks to keep it healthy.

Electional–a method of choosing the best moment for any important event.

Physiognomical–deals with those facial characteristics held to be under a particular star's influence.

18

♈	Aries	☉	Sun
♉	Taurus	☽	Moon
♊	Gemini	☿	Mercury
♋	Cancer	♀	Venus
♌	Leo	♂	Mars
♍	Virgo	♃	Jupiter
♎	Libra	♄	Saturn
♏	Scorpio	♅	Uranus
♐	Sagittarius	♆	Neptune
♑	Capricorn	♇	Pluto
♒	Aquarius		
♓	Pisces		

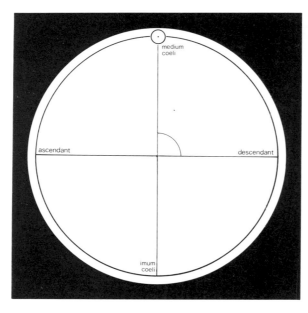

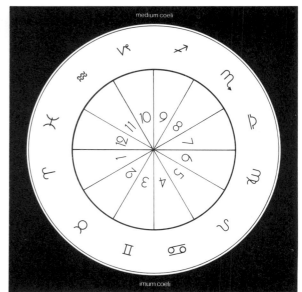

Above:
The signs of the zodiac and the planets with their symbols.

Above right:
The ecliptic with ascendant, medium coeli, descendant, and imum coeli.

Above, far right:
The twelve signs of the zodiac around the ecliptic, each in its natural house.

Pages 22 and 23:
Saturn presiding over Aquarius and Capricorn (left) and the Moon presiding over Cancer (right). Miniatures from 'De Sphaera', a fifteenth-century Italian manuscript. Biblioteca Estense, Modena.

The twelve signs of the zodiac from 'De Astrorum Scientia' by Leopold of Austria (Augsburg, 1489).

Ecliptic—the apparent path of the sun in the heavens which during the year describes a great circle from west to east.

Zodiac—an imaginary belt in the sky spreading about eight degrees either side of the ecliptic. The principal planets travel along it at different speeds. Traditional European astrology divides this sphere into twelve equal parts of thirty degrees each. These are the signs of the zodiac.

Signs of the Zodiac—named after the constellations, thus: Aries, Taurus, Gemini, Cancer, Leo, Virgo, Libra, Scorpio, Sagittarius, Capricorn, Aquarius, and Pisces. However, these twelve divisions no longer correspond to the constellations sharing their name because of the:

Precession of the Equinoxes—the equinox (when day and night are of equal length because the sun crosses the plane of the earth's equator) never occurs in exactly the same place two years running. The spot moves gradually round the sky taking about 26,000 years to complete its circuit. The First Point of Aries is the beginning of the zodiac, and this moves backwards around the heavens at the same rate, taking the belt of signs with it. Consequently the date of the sun's entry into each constellation no longer corresponds to the dates still used by astrologers, which are based on calculations made by the Ancient Greeks. For instance, the sun now goes into Cancer in July, and not June, and Cancer now covers the constellation of Gemini. Yet a person born under Cancer is still given the same characteristics as prescribed by tradition. As Michel Gauquelin so eloquently puts it in his *Astrology and Science* '. . . the old lodgers have moved but their names are still on the doors.' This is one of the chief arguments which sceptics level at astrologers.

Planets—the ancients included the sun and moon among these and based their order on what they imagined to be their respective distances from earth, which they regarded as the centre of the universe, thus: Moon, Mercury, Venus, Sun, Mars, Jupiter, and Saturn. The new planets are Uranus, discovered 1781, Neptune discovered 1846, and Pluto, not discovered until 1930. While modern astrologers know the universe is not geocentric, they still perform their calculations as if it were—once again a matter of tradition.

Houses—Every twenty-four hours the earth turns on its axis. As the stars seem to travel across the heavens in that time astrologers treated one day as a miniature year and divided the daily motion of the stars into twelve houses. They are numbered in an opposite direction to the planets' motions, and the first house is at the ascendant (*see* below). While the houses remain constant the signs of the zodiac move. The ecliptic has been compared with a clock face. The signs move all the time like the two hands, but the houses stay still like the numbers.

Ascendant—the degree of the zodiac rising on the eastern horizon at the time of birth. In horoscopes this is usually taken as the sign that is rising.

Cusp—The lines dividing the houses. Not always as simple as it sounds since not all astrologers agree about house divisions.

Medium Coeli (M.C)—mid-heaven: when from the observer's standpoint the sun appears at its meridian at noon.

Imum Coeli (I.C)—the exact opposite. A line drawn between these two points intersects at right angles the horizontal line linking ascend-

ant in the east and descendant in the west. This cross forms the angles.

Angles—planets on or near these four lines have greater significance.

Transit—on a horoscope are a number of special or 'sensitive' spots, *e.g.*, the ascendant degree. A planet passing over this place is 'transiting' it, so the astrologer, who possesses tables to show the movements of the planets, can indicate what sort of influences may be felt during a transit, and whether such times would be good or otherwise for particular enterprises, health, wealth and love. These may be worked out from the revolution of the sun.

Revolution of the Sun—a yearly horoscope or anniversary chart drawn for the hour and day when the sun was at the place it occupied at the individual's birth.

Aspects—a line drawn from the centre of the earth to one planet and another line linked to some other planet so that the angle between may be measured.

Opposition—when a planet is rising at 180 degrees from a setting planet. This is usually considered 'bad' or 'difficult'.

Conjunction—when two planets are within 8 or 10 degrees of each other. Depending on the planets involved, this aspect can be good or bad.

Sextile—two planets 60 degrees apart. A good aspect.

Square—two planets 90 degrees apart. A bad aspect.

Trine—two planets 120 degrees apart. Very good, even if any of the planets involved are regarded as traditionally unfriendly.

Minor Aspects:

Quintile—72 degrees.

Sesquadrate—135 degrees.

Quincunx—150 degrees.

Orb—the margin allowed by astrologers: around 7 degrees for sextile, and 12 degrees for conjunction or opposition of sun and moon. If the aspects had to be absolutely accurate they would not occur so often—hence the orb.

Ephemeris—a reference book found in libraries and bookshops which shows the position of sun, moon, planets, and certain stars in the solar system at any particular time. It may also include a table of houses.

Table of Houses—by which the astrologer makes adjustments, depending on the location of an individual's birthplace.

Sidereal Time (S.T)—found in the ephemeris, and measured not by the sun, which is clock time, but by the stars. The time is calculated as how long it takes the earth to rotate once on its axis using a particular star as reference point. A sidereal day is about 4 minutes shorter than a solar day, so there are slightly more than 366 of these days in a year.

Horoscope—literally 'that which looks at the hour'. A chart that shows the position of the planets, sun and moon at the time of birth. It may be regarded as a still photograph of the heavens. A horoscope is relatively easy to learn to draw in a mechanical sort of way, but interpreting it requires skill, practice, and not a little intuition. Remember it is always drawn from a geocentric viewpoint.

Left:
As an example of physiognomical astrology wrinkles on the forehead are said to be signs of the influence of certain planets.

Bottom left:
An illustration of the symptoms of syphilis, which was blamed on the conjunction of Jupiter and Saturn in Scorpio.

The symbols used by astrologers to denote certain important aspects, together with examples of planetary aspects.

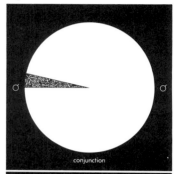

conjunction

opposition

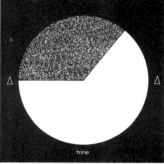

trine

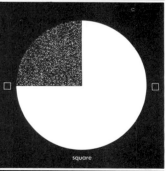

square

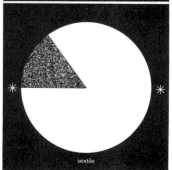

sextile

21

Saturno huomini tardi et rei produce
Rubaduri et buxiardi et assasini
Villani et uili et senza alchuna luce
Pastori et zoppi et simili meschini :·

· LVNA ·

La luna al nauigar molto conforta
Et in peschare et ucellare et caccia
A tuti i suoy figliuoli apre la porta
Et anche al solazzare che ad altri piaccia

The Ancient World

Mesopotamia

The earliest records show that astrology was born in Mesopotamia. This ancient plain lies between two great slow-moving rivers—the Tigris and the Euphrates. Here is modern Iraq, and although the vast area may look drab and uninspiring this is one of the earliest cradles of civilized man. The entire region might be looked on as a gigantic and mysterious palimpsest of civilizations. Each one flourished as if it must reign forever, and obscured what had gone before, only to be replaced and shrouded in its turn.

Here dwelt Sumerians, Akkadians, Babylonians, Assyrians, Persians and Seleucids—and a whole host of others. Read the Old Testament, and you will recognize some of the peoples, kingdoms, and cities of Mesopotamia: the Tower of Babel that provoked God's wrath; Babylon, the city of the Israelites' captivity, where Daniel bested not only the lions but also King Nebuchadnezzar's astrologers, stargazers, Chaldeans and priests in the skill of dream interpretation; and Ur of the Chaldees, the alleged birthplace of the patriarch Abraham. Incidentally, Islamic history has it that when the ancient astrologers read the heavens for the year of Abraham's birth they saw that a child would eventually destroy the supremacy of their religion. The king, Nimrod (that mighty hunter), was not taking any risks, and so ordered all newborn babies to be slaughtered, but Abraham's mother hid her son in a cave. When Abraham's religion grew powerful the arrogant Nimrod built a tall tower and climbed up so that he might see this god of Abraham's.

The facts behind the Bible stories and their relationship with Muslim traditions do not concern us here, but the places mentioned definitely existed, as archaeologists have proved over the last 100 years. Now, ancient stones and fragments of artefacts may be of absorbing interest only to antiquarians, but we should try to imbue the faint ghosts of their creators with the life which they once possessed in full measure, remembering that their ideas are still the foundation of that astrology practised in the western world.

Irrigation produced fertile plains, suitable for consolidating tribes of nomadic herdsmen into a nation of urban societies. The clear, dry climate presented ample opportunities for observing the skies and for making Mesopotamia the ideal birthplace for those Siamese twins astronomy and astrology. Even when a subject is veiled in legend and ambiguity there is always some practical aspect in its origins, and the Roman writer Cicero put the beginnings of astrology in perspective when he wrote in *De Divinatione*: 'The Egyptians and Babylonians reside in vast plains where no mountains obstruct their view of the entire hemisphere, and so they have applied themselves to that kind of divination called astrology . . .'

With justifiable hindsight we might also

Stele of King Ashurbanipal of Assyria. His extensive library of cuneiform tablets has provided posterity with much information about Babylonian astrology. British Museum, London.

add: '. . . to that kind of science called astronomy,' for it was several thousand years before the twins could be separated.

The earliest civilization to leave its indelible, if mysterious, prints on the face of Mesopotamia was that of the Sumerians—a non-Semitic people who originated on the Iranian plateau, and settled in southern Mesopotamia around 5000 years B.C.

By 3500 B.C. these remarkably sophisticated Sumerians were using chariot, plough, and potter's wheel, and had evolved a literate urban society. Their chief cities were Ur, Kish, and Erech, and the most unusual feature of these cities was the ziggurat—a combination of temple, administrative offices, and grain storehouse. It was square in ground plan, with high walls inclining inwards, and its flat summit was used by the priests for observing the skies. It has been suggested the Sumerians originally built these 'mock mountains' because of their mountain-dwelling ancestors. Whatever the precise reason—and we can be sure they had one —the top of the ziggurat provided the important meeting point between heaven and earth.

We have to try to understand that religion and what we loosely term 'science' were indivisible among those early civilizations. After all, the deities were considered responsible for causing many of the phenomena science has since explained to us. By studying the heavens the priest-astrologer-scientist was not only communing with the heavenly bodies, which he believed were close enough to touch, but also measuring the movement of time. The seasons had to be marked carefully if the religious rituals were to be performed at the correct times, and agriculture obviously depended on an accurate prediction of the rising and flooding of the two great rivers. From the information gathered the priests must have attempted to work out a comprehensive code for the needs of their society.

The most famous Sumerian invention was cuneiform—the earliest form of writing, consisting of wedge-shaped symbols scratched on to soft clay tablets with a pointed stick or stylus. Thus, Sumerian is the first recorded language, but oddly enough one unrelated to any other. Although conquest made this tongue a well-and-truly dead one, the ancient cuneiform texts were fortunately preserved and copied for religious and educational purposes by successive civilizations until the beginning of the Christian era. In the nineteenth century scholars managed to decipher Sumerian, because the Akkadian conquerors of Sumer had compiled dictionaries. Since Akkadian is a Semitic language the translations were intelligible—at least to the informed. The later inhabitants of Mesopotamia, as well as Persians and Hittites, adopted cuneiform writing, and it was used by differing languages until the coming of Christianity. It is from these curious markings on the small baked clay tablets that we gain our knowledge of the dawn of astrology, as well as much about ancient customs and beliefs.

In 2350 B.C. the Akkadians overran Sumer and ruled all Mesopotamia. They worshipped the sun, moon, and the planet Venus, but they regarded the sun as female, while the other two were male. The Sumerians had worshipped a whole pantheon of gods, but the mingling of the two religious and cultures changed the sun into a male deity called Shamash. He was the son of the moon, Sin, an old man rowing a boat across the heavens. The beautiful star Venus was assigned a dual role: in the evening it was the female Ishtar, the goddess of fertility, and in the morning the male Ishtar, the god of war.

The fabulous Babylon was the chief city of Babylonia, the next great Semitic state to build upon Sumerian roots. Since this civilization had the most pronounced influence upon early astrology a brief history may help to clarify certain stages in the development of the reading of the heavens, especially when we understand that Babylonia's several conquerors continued and extended existing traditions.

The first Babylonian dynasty flourished between 1830 and 1530 B.C., and its most renowned king, Hammurabi, reigned between 1728 and 1686 B.C. Tempted by Babylon's power and wealth, the Hittites and Kassites constantly attacked until the fourteenth century B.C. when the Assyrians conquered Babylonia.

Babylonian Boundary stone, c. 1120 B.C. The zodiac took many centuries to evolve, some of the signs, such as the Scorpion on this stone, being created by the Babylonians. British Museum, London.

25

Babylonian boundary stone, c. 1200 B.C., showing a king and his daughter before a goddess, with Venus, the Moon, and the Sun above. These were for the Babylonians not only planets but gods to be worshipped, placated, and observed. Musée du Louvre, Paris.

New Babylon—the Chaldean Empire—with its king, Nebuchadnezzar. To judge from the Book of Daniel the writer did not think too highly of the king's skygazing advisers, for Daniel was set above them since his God-inspired powers could solve problems beyond the reach of their lesser talents. In Isaiah the Hebrew prophet proclaiming God's dire judgement on 'the lady Babylon' showed no admiration for the astrologers' skills: 'Let now the astrologers, the stargazers, the monthly prognosticators stand up, and save thee from these things that shall come upon thee. Behold they shall be as stubble; the fire shall burn them; they shall not deliver themselves from the power of the flame . . .'

While not wanting to argue with Holy Writ one should regard this denigration as somewhat partisan, for those much-maligned stargazers certainly warrant our admiration when we learn that around 380 B.C. Kidinnu, a Chaldean astronomer, calculated the length of a lunar month as 29 days, 12 hours, 44 minutes and 3.3 seconds. Modern science sets it at 29 days, 12 hours, 44 minutes, and 2.87 seconds. This was remarkably accurate and painstaking stargazing on the part of the Babylonians, who had no equipment more sophisticated than the clepsydra and gnomon.

Between 538 and 330 B.C. the Persians dominated the ancient world. After them came Alexander the Great and the Greek influence, which is as far as this history lesson need go in relation to astrology.

Since the Babylonians believed that everything in the world had some meaning and was related in some way to everything else, all nature had to be studied and records kept of every kind of phenomenon. The priests interpreted and listed dreams, studied the entrails of animals, formulated theories on abnormal births, and recorded the regular or sudden appearances of birds, insects and animals, but above all they watched the movements of the celestial bodies. We have to try to understand that this was not so much an accumulation of superstitious magic as an attempt to interpret the whole of life within the limits of the age in which they lived.

The Enuma Anu Enlil tablets are a collection of omens and observations concerning the skies and dating back to the first dynasty. They record mainly eclipses, shapes and quarters of the moon, and if there was a halo around it. There are plenty of what would now be called meteorological and farming forecasts: 'If the moon has a halo it will be wet or cloudy'. 'If it thunders in the month of Shebat there will be a plague of locusts.' 'If the storm god Adad thunders in the month of Nisannu, the small barley crop will lessen.'

Eclipses were considered particularly hazardous as is shown in this communication found in the archives of Nineveh from a priest to King Ashurbanipal: 'To my Lord the King of all Countries from your servant Bel-u. May the gods, Bel, Nabu and Shamash bless your Majesty. If an eclipse occurs but is not observed in the capital such an eclipse is considered not to have happened. The capital means the city in which

The Assyrians were undoubtedly a fierce people, but perhaps their Babylonian conquest helped to civilize them, for they did nothing to erase existing astrological practices. Indeed, they continued and developed them. Later centuries —including our own—should be particularly grateful to one of Assyria's famous kings, the antiquarian Ashurbanipal (668–626 B.C.). His library not only stored contemporary records but collected and copied those which by then were ancient history. It is from this host of cuneiform tablets that we have acquired much of our knowledge of Babylonian law, medicine, religion, poetry, astronomy, and astrology.

Around 600 B.C., after a series of independent rulers had helped the Medes and Persians to overthrow Assyrian supremacy, there arose the

the king is staying. Now there were clouds everywhere: we thus do not know whether the eclipse occurred or not. The Lord of all Kings should write to Assur and to all cities such as Babylon, Nippur, Uruk and Borsippa.' These were obviously cities with established astronomers. He goes on: 'Possibly it was observed in these cities . . . I have already written everything to your majesty about the portents of an eclipse that happened in the months Adarru and Nisannu. And as to the apotropaic [the turning away of evil] rites for the eclipse that are already performed, what harm can be done if there was none? It is profitable to perform the rites. The king should not send the ritual experts away. The great gods who live in the city of your majesty have covered up the sky and not shown the eclipse. That is what the king should know; that this eclipse has no relation to your majesty or his country. On this count the king should be happy . . .'

Even after all this time the interchange of correspondence between astrologers and rulers makes fascinating reading: very human blends of caution, fallibility, and triumph at being proved right!

Predictions relating to the political affairs of neighbouring countries were also recorded. Unlike that of later centuries Babylonian astrology was mundane. Since the government of Babylon was theocratic—ruled by those who claimed to have divine knowledge—such power was hardly to be used to predict the fortunes of ordinary men. Thus, it was essential for the

Babylonian zodiac. The ancients marked the route of the sun and moon by thirty-six constellations from which they selected twelve chiefs. Some of these are the ancestors of the traditional zodiac.

became the foundation of religious calendars not only for the Babylonians but also for the Assyrians, Jews, Aramaeans, and Phoenicians.

We cannot divorce astronomy from astrology if we want to understand how the Babylonians read the skies, and their most famous collection of astronomical data comes from the Mulapin Tablets (the name means 'Plough Star'), probably written around 700 B.C., but which contains the results of studies going back another 600 years.

From these we learn that the Babylonians divided the sky into three sections: the Way of Anu—the god of the sky—which corresponds with what the Greeks called the ecliptic and later the zodiac; the Way of Enlil—god of the atmosphere—roughly corresponding to the Tropic of Cancer; and the Way of Ea—god of the ocean depths—roughly corresponding to the Tropic of Capricorn.

Shamash and Sin followed a similar road called 'the Way in relation to Anu', and the Babylonians noticed that on their journey these major luminaries traversed certain constellations of stars, and they carefully recorded when certain stars rose and set. From their vivid mythology they gave the constellations names of strange creatures, many of which are still with us; for instance, a huge lion, a scorpion, a goat with a fishtail (Capricorn), and hippo-centaurs (Sagittarius) . . . To mark the route of the sun and moon with greater precision thirty-six of the brightest stars were chosen from the constellations. These were termed 'counsellors', and they watched over both men and heavens. From them were selected twelve seasonal 'chiefs', who ruled the constellations through which the sun and moon regularly travelled. The portions of the sky superintended by the 'chiefs' were called 'berous'.

These berous are the ancestors of our twelve signs of the zodiac, although the real zodiac—as as we know it—did not come into existence until after the seventh century B.C. Not all our twelve signs necessarily sprang from Babylonian tradition: some must have arisen as the result of Mesopotamian ideas merging with later Greek and perhaps Egyptian mythology. Experts seem unable to decide on this, or to pin down the exact date when the twelve familiar signs were first used. However, by the time the Assyrians appeared on the scene, some of the usual signs and constellation names existed, such as Leo, Capricorn, Scorpio, Sagittarius, and Taurus (then at the spring equinox).

priest-astronomer-astrologer to scan the sky and earth for every conceivable omen in order to advise the ruler on national and domestic policy. Our concept of the special birthday horoscope—even for a ruler—did not occur until the end of the Chaldean empire.

The priests kept constant vigil with the heavens from the flat summits of ziggurats—one of which may well have been the notorious Tower of Babel. The Babylonian ziggurat was a square-based, pyramid-shaped watchtower, made up of a succession of painted terraces reaching to around 300 feet in height. This must have been the most important building in all major cities—apart from the king's palaces—for it also housed a temple, stores of grain against famine, and what we would call government offices. One can imagine that the priests really did feel they stood on the threshold of heaven and earth in their eyries above the dust and noise of the cities.

But what was it these Babylonian stargazers sought in the skies, and how did they marshal and interpret their information? First and foremost we must remember that these ancient people were religious—otherwise a theocracy would not have been feasible. We would regard them as superstitious, just as later ages will see some of our customs as amusing or meaningless. Many days were considered unlucky for work, enjoyment, or even taking particular medicines, so it was important to know when such days began. Calculations were based on the moon, each quarter being regarded as a holy and therefore unpropitious day. The Babylonians divided their day into twelve hours, and counted the beginning of the month and week from the evening when the new moon appeared. This somewhat erratic lunar calendar

Naturally, such observant people could not fail to wonder at the five visible planets. Unlike the myriad glittering fixed stars these moved. Sometimes they seemed to go faster or even backwards and therefore they must be considered especially significant. The Babylonians called the planets 'wild goats' as opposed to the tame and tethered variety, and saw them as 'interpreters' because their movements were held to predict definite future events.

Each planet was the dwelling of one of the existing gods. This was not chosen arbitrarily, but demonstrated a clever fusion of observation and imagination. The relationship was based on the planet's closely observed characteristics, which corresponded with those already deeply embedded in the beliefs surrounding the respective deity.

Ishtar, the goddess of fertility, dwelt, not surprisingly, in the lovely evening star: the planet Venus. Marduk (Baal), chief of the gods, dwelt in Jupiter, which was considered the chief planet, since it appeared to wander least from the Way of Anu. The king of gods was not exactly predictable or totally benign since he could send storms and other catastrophes. Nergal, the threatening and malevolent god of war, naturally lived on the red planet Mars. Ninurta, an aging, chillier version of Marduk, lived on the remote and flickering Saturn. Although though to be a distant and pensive god, he was still to be feared since he might send storms or pleasant breezes. Nabu lived on Mercury. Because this planet's proximity to the sun makes it hard to keep under surveillance, the god was given a lot of uncomplimentary titles: 'the enemy', 'the stubborn one', 'the fox', and 'the leopard'. Depending on each planet's appearance and position, the particular gods were either going to show kindness or quite the reverse.

A prediction concerning the king's child demonstrates how the Babylonians regarded these planets, which they revered even more than Shamash and Sin: 'If a child is born when Venus rises, his life will be calm and pleasurable; wherever he goes he will be loved; his days shall be long.' Alternatively: 'If a child is born when Jupiter is rising and Mars is setting, he will have happiness, and will see the downfall of his enemy.' However, and here note the difference in planetary positions: 'If a child is born when Mars is rising and Jupiter setting, later on the hand of his enemy will take him captive.'

At the centre of this celestial government stood the priest-astrologer, who could not control the signs in the sky, but had the special skill to interpret them.

Greece

Geography conditions cultural patterns. Ideas cannot be transplanted to a wholly different environment without being altered. Whereas the important rivers of Mesopotamia made it necessary for one strong ruler and religion to maintain power in the region, the scattered city-states of the Greek mainland and islands made such rigid unity impossible. Stargazing never became a priestly concern, but one for the secular scientist and philosopher. Moreover the tradition that the stars spoke only about the fate of king and state had no place in Greek society. So it was in Greece that genethlialogy developed, and this practice naturally popularized and spread the belief in astrology.

While Babylonian astrology-astronomy concerned itself chiefly with reading omens and compiling a calendar, the Greek thinkers tried to relate what happened in the heavens to the order of the entire universe—to incorporate it into their abstractions on the meaning of existence. To this end they made use of their undoubted mathematical genius in order to calculate the relationship between everything

Assyrian astrolabe used for making astrological calculations.

The fertility goddess, Ishtar, whom the Babylonians linked with the planet Venus. Statue of the third century B.C. Musée du Louvre, Paris.

29

The ruins of Babylon, once the mighty capital of Mesopotamia. In 1750 B.C. under Hammurabi it became the centre of the Babylonian Empire. Destroyed in 699, it was rebuilt in the reign of Nebuchadnezzar.

Opposite page:
The Ishtar Gate at Babylon. This 'wicked city' of the Bible was one of the cradles of astrology. Staatliche Museen, Berlin.

Aristotle, the most famous of the Greek philosophers and a pupil of Plato, believed that the movements of the planets affected what took place on earth. Bust. Museo Capitolino, Rome.

they saw. It is unlikely this mathematical skill sprang up in isolation, and experts consider the Greeks must have built on at least some Babylonian foundations.

Although Greek mathematical astronomy did not really begin before the fifth century B.C. we can be sure that farmers and sailors had long been watching the skies to gather information pertaining to their livelihoods. However, this had none of the precision of Babylon, or its centuries of recorded phenomena. The Greeks did not differentiate between planets and fixed stars until the fifth century B.C., and our word planet comes from the Greek *planetes*, which means 'wanderer'.

Some modern astrologers still claim Thales of Miletus (624–565 B.C.), the earliest Greek scientist, to be the first to spread astrology among his countrymen, but this seems doubtful, since his interest in the heavens and the prediction of the eclipse arose from scientific study rather than any intuitive and 'magical' approach.

The brilliance and complexity of Greek thought which had so much influence in the

31

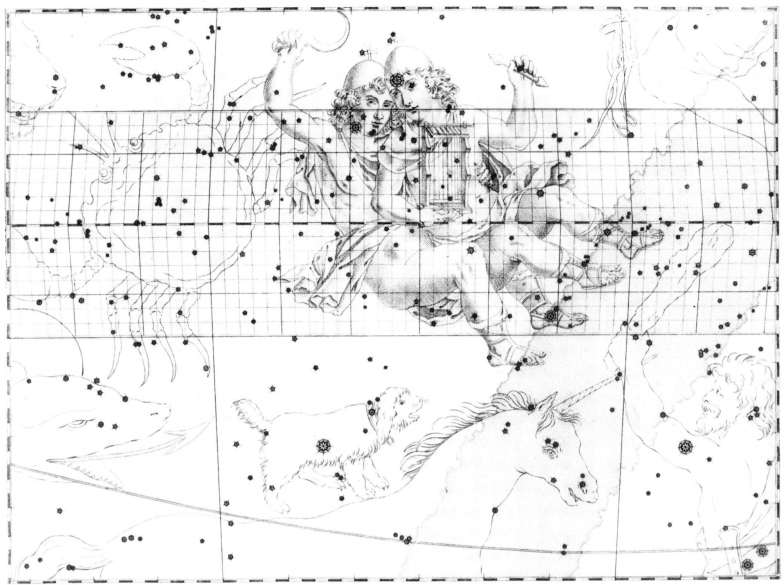

An eighteenth-century star map showing the ancient Greek personification of the Gemini, who were seen as the twin gods Castor and Pollux.

west, where for many centuries it was regarded as almost sacrosanct, had a paradoxical effect on the knowledge of the heavens. It retarded astronomy and popularized astrology at what might be called the unscientific or imaginative level. The more superstitious theories were born from the abstractions of the great philosophers, which gave them weight and respectability. That specious or unthinking minds trivialized many of these ideas beyond recognition is not the fault of their originators. However, the contact of astrology with philosophy ended by making the whole subject a highly complex one.

Before obtaining some idea of how the personalized horoscope came into being, it is worthwhile glancing at some of the great thinkers who influenced the course of astrology.

In the sixth century B.C. Pythagoras and his followers saw the universe in much the same terms as the Babylonians: a whole made up of interrelating parts. Like them he declared it to be geocentric. Curiously enough, in the third century B.C., another Greek, Aristarchus, a very precise observer, put forward the theory of a heliocentric universe. Nobody accepted this, and nearly 2000 years were to elapse before Copernicus propounded the same idea. Certainly, Pythagoras was probably the first man to believe the world to be spherical, but he was a mystic as well as a mathematician, and the brotherhood he founded saw the key to under-

standing the universe in numbers. His theory of celestial order makes a pleasing geometrical and aesthetic concept. The Pythagorean scale consists of seven notes on a heavenly lyre. These are the seven planets, including sun and moon, and pitch depends on their respective distances from earth. The planets and the fixed stars are attached to spheres which revolve around the earth in concentric circles.

Plato (429–347 B.C.) upheld this Pythagorean view of the order of things which control earthly existence. In his work *Timaeus*, which is concerned with cosmology, he points out the eight powers as being the sun, the moon, the fixed stars, and the five planets. For Plato there were vibrations and harmonies between souls on earth and what took place in the sky in which they originated.

Aristotle (382–322 B.C.) further emphasized these ideas, for he claimed that our world must be connected with what transpired in the upper world, and therefore all terrestrial power was controlled by these movements.

Such philosophical ideas stress an innate need to relate man to the entire universe. The uncertainty of the times may well have helped to spread the belief in astrology among the Greeks. Most people—no matter how democratic in intention—do not really like being complete masters of their destiny. This seems like too much freedom, too much responsibility, and so they look to the powers above to bring them fortune or to blame when things go wrong.

Numerous wars among the small city-states destroyed the cohesion of society. While the intellectuals turned to obscure and elite philosophical sects, ordinary people—as is frequently the case in troubled ages—fell back on superstition and magic, eagerly absorbing the unusual doctrines and practices of other regions. The conquests of Alexander the Great extended Greek influence, but also brought back home ideas from Mesopotamia and elsewhere. These ancient Eastern concepts fell on fertile Greek ground and flourished to produce a hybrid plant.

The book that probably contributed most to spreading Babylonian astrology among the Greeks was the *Babyloniaca*, written in Greek around 280 B.C. by Berosus, a Chaldean priest from the temple of Marduk in Babylon. In three volumes he narrated the history of his people, and devoted a large section of it to describing their astrological traditions. Being a priest meant that Berosus was also an astrologer-astronomer, so he understood his subject. Writing in Greek assured him a wide and enthusiastic readership. At last, a vast and detailed source of celestial data from Babylonian archives was available to the would-be Greek astrologer. From then on, western astrology didn't look back, or rather, it so looked forward it almost lost touch with its roots. Success caused Berosus to settle on the island of Cos, where there was a small, rich Greek colony and the medical school of Hippocrates. There he taught astrology, and since some of his pupils were also studying medicine, astrology and healing became closely allied, and remained so until the seventeenth century.

By the second century B.C. the practice of reading the stars to predict the future had spread as far as Rome, where a number of astrological manuals were in circulation. *The Revelations of Nechepso and Petosiris* was particularly popular, and suggests that the compilers of that age were not above a piece of clever merchandising, for the work purported to be written by a fictional Egyptian pharaoh. At that time Egypt, under Hellenic influence, was gaining a reputation for expertise in astrology.

It was also in the second century B.C. that a startling scientific discovery was made by Hipparchus, the most famous of the ancient Greek astronomers. This was the precession of the equinoxes—the first point of Aries had moved back all the way along the constellation of Pisces. At that time, of course, astrologers were not to understand that this fact made nonsense of the rules they were establishing, nor were they to know that it would provide twentieth-century sceptics with one of the best arguments against their ancient art. Indeed, modern astrologers evade this issue, for the most part, by claiming the stars are 'signs' rather than actual 'causes'.

Naturally, the Chaldean tradition had to be transformed before it became the foundation of the astrology we are familiar with today, and it was the Greeks who carried out this transformation. They too had a pantheon full of gods, and could hardly be expected to relinquish their religion and culture in favour of those of the Babylonians, and so they set about finding equivalents. Where some seemed unsuitable they altered Babylonian lore to fit in with their own.

For the Greeks the moon was ever female, and so the male Sin became Selene. Helios, her father, took over from Shamash, the Babylonian sungod. The gods of love and war presented little problem: Ishtar and Nergal became respectively Aphrodite and Ares. Marduk's temperament, however, did not fit in with that of Zeus, king of the Greek gods, and so the renamed planet became benign and tolerant. Ninurta became Kronos: still the aging, dethroned king, but a wise old fellow, a little bad-tempered and moody, but less fierce than his Babylonian counterpart. The 'foxy' Nabu became Hermes, and lost his unflattering titles, for the Greeks admired this god, and thought of him as 'crafty' rather than cunning and deceitful.

Each 'wanderer' became embellished with the multitudinous characteristics of the presiding deity and, with its allotted interests and attributes, controlled a separate area of man's destiny. Aphrodite and Zeus were the great 'benefics', while Ares and Kronos were the 'malefics'. All these centuries later such traits have not radically altered in the eyes of astrologers. (For a detailed description of the planets' influences see the final chapter on the signs of the zodiac.)

With the spreading popularity of astrology the stargazers could not simply look skywards and declare a general fate for everyone, but had to devise a method suitable for the individual.

Aphrodite, the Greek goddess of love, became associated with the planet Venus, when the astrology of the Chaldeans spread to Greece. Rhodes Museum.

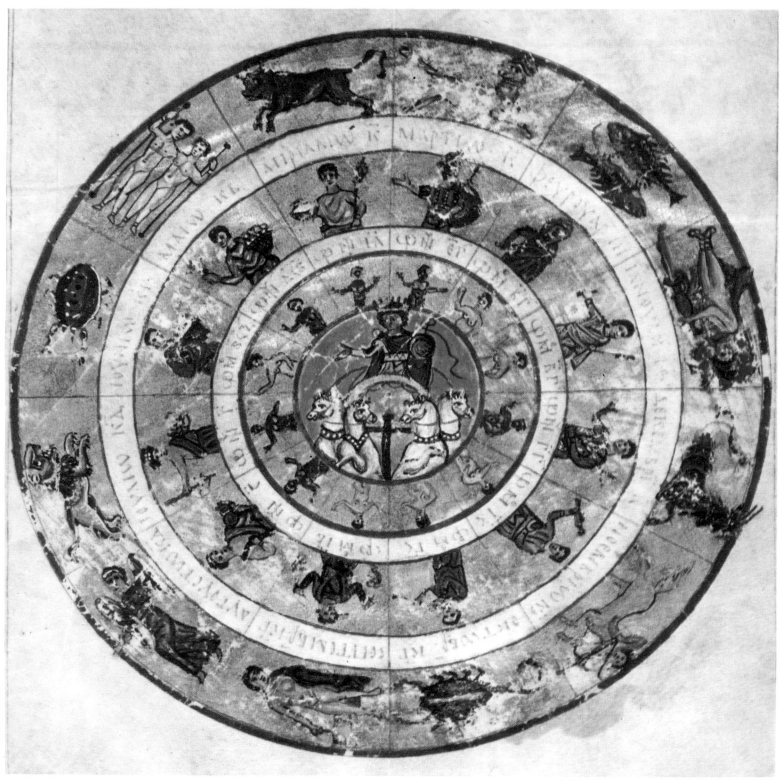

An illustration to Ptolemy's famous 'Tetrabiblos' showing the sun and the signs of the zodiac. Byzantine, A.D. 820. Biblioteca Apostolica, Vatican.

They deemed the most momentous happening in any person's life to be birth, and so based their predictions on the state of the sky at the time of birth. At first this may have been a straightforward matter of deciding that a child's future would be influenced by whichever stars rose on the day of birth. However, a more precise form of prediction had to be invented if the futures of all the children born on any one day were going to differ. So it was that the personal horoscope came into being, based on the degree of the ecliptic rising above the eastern horizon at the exact moment of birth.

Instead of surveying all the heavens Greek astrologers chose to study the old Way of Anu, which gives us the present-day path of the zodiac. Zodiac comes from the word *zodiakos* meaning 'to do with animals', derived from *zoidon* meaning 'little animals', perhaps painted or carved. By now there were the twelve regular

signs we know today marking this path in sections of thirty degrees. Those of Babylonian origin wore Greek faces, and were given relationships in Greek mythology.

The Greek mind was fascinated by mathematics and complicated theories, all of which adds to the difficulty of working out the scheme in the heavens, as well as our understanding of it. The Greeks regarded the twenty-four-hour day as a microcosm of a year, and divided it into twelve houses (remember that the houses are nothing to do with the signs), each of which was given a separate and detailed meaning that has not basically altered over the ages.

To make it even more difficult from the layman's point of view, Greek astrology lovingly worked out mathematical correspondences between the aspects of the planets in the various houses. There was a reason why some angles

were considered favourable, and others were not: for instance the sextile resembled the pleasing hexagonal cells made by bees! However, many of the obscure motives behind these rules are either lost to the modern mind, or beyond its comprehension, and so the doctrine became arbitrary.

Apart from the planets' geometrical relationship to one another, they were also affected by the constellations they crossed. In some they 'rejoiced', while in others they felt 'in exile'. For instance, the sun is discontented in Libra because he is approaching winter, but happy in Leo because it is summer.

The ancients believed that the signs were ruled by particular planets, which greatly influenced their characteristics. The reasoning behind who rules what is not too complicated to guess at when we see that the times of greatest light and warmth, Cancer and Leo, are governed by the moon and sun, bringers of light and heat. The two opposite signs, Capricorn and Aquarius, belong to Saturn, because this planet, being furthest from the sun, must be the coldest. Saturn's neighbour, Jupiter, rules Sagittarius and Pisces. The one next to it is Mars, which rules Scorpio and Aries. Mercury is never further than one sign from the sun in either direction, and so rules Gemini and Virgo, while Venus, never being further than two signs on either side of the sun, rules Libra and Taurus.

Obviously Uranus, Pluto and Neptune cannot be included among the above, since they were not discovered until long after the ancients' rules had become a tradition. Thus they became joint-rulers with some of the original planets: Uranus also governs Aquarius, Neptune governs Pisces, and Pluto rules Scorpio.

The Greeks divided the zodiac into various

A Roman astrological globe with various figures representing the constellations.

groupings. Quadruplicities and triplicities (also called trigons) are still regarded as of special significance by astrologers.

Quadruplicities refer to the three qualities, namely, cardinal, fixed, and mutable.

Cardinal: Aries, Cancer, Libra, Capricorn.

Fixed: Leo, Scorpio, Taurus, Aquarius.

Mutable: Gemini, Virgo, Sagittarius, Pisces.

The motivation behind such divisions appears simple: the cardinal signs mark the beginnings of each of the four seasons; the fixed signs show when the sun is firmly established in those seasons; and the mutable signs occur when an old season is in the process of giving way to a new one.

Triplicities relate to the four elements, which are as follows:

Fire: Aries, Leo, Sagittarius.

Earth: Taurus, Virgo, Capricorn.

Air: Gemini, Libra, Aquarius.

Water: Cancer, Scorpio, Pisces.

Once again for the meanings behind these groups, and the effects of their planets the reader must refer to the chapter devoted to the zodiac.

Other groupings of signs in which the ancients saw particular significance included male and female, single and double, earth and water, and human and animal. Ptolemy, the great geographer and savant, who lived about A.D. 140, and was the writer of one of the most comprehensive works on astrology which influenced the ancient world, specified four groupings: solstitial for Cancer and Capricorn; equinoctial for Aries and Libra; solid for Taurus, Leo, Scorpio and Aquarius; and bicorporeal for Gemini, Virgo, Sagittarius, and Pisces. The reasoning behind the first two looks clear enough, but the last two remain obscure.

Now we can see how far the Greeks had travelled from the mundane astrology of Babylon. Using imagination, observation, philosophy, and mathematics they succeeded in turning the practice of reading the stars into something very complex indeed, which eventually left it open not only to various interpretation but also to the subjective dogma of charlatans of later ages.

Egypt

The Egyptians had studied the heavens since the beginnings of their great civilization, but they were more interested in compiling a seasonal calendar to predict floodings of the Nile for agricultural purposes, than in reading omens among the stars. Astrology probably did not reach Egypt until the end of the reign of the great pharaohs, and must have spread from Babylonian sources.

Signs of the zodiac discovered at Dendera suggested at first that these astrological symbols actually originated in Egypt, but later it was realized that they did not date back further than the Roman era. In fact, the zodiac does not appear to have reached Egypt before the third century B.C. By this time a fusion of Chaldean, Greek and Egyptian astrological ideas must have occurred in the great centres of cultural interchange such as Alexandria.

By Roman times, Egypt had become one of the foremost places for the study of astrology, and the Egyptians did much to foster the idea that the practice had grown up in the shadow of the pyramids. But, in order to keep the record straight, we must realize that what some writers called the Egyptian system of astrology was in fact the Greek planetary one, and the eternal tables on which the Egyptians were thought to have collected their ancient star lore were compiled from Babylonian writings.

Ptolemy

Ptolemy was a Greek, born near Alexandria, and it was in that city he wrote his *Tetrabiblos*, still thought of as one of the great gospels of astrology, for it contained all the information of past ages. This famous cartographer and geographer added further weight to the geocentric tradition. He considered astrology to be useful for two reasons: knowledge of the future could make a person accept his fate; and such foreknowledge might help an individual to avoid particular pitfalls lying ahead.

Like many later astrologers, Ptolemy faced the dilemma of just when life began. Was it at birth, or the moment of conception? Ideally, he felt, conception was the real beginning, but, since this would be almost impossible to calculate in most cases, he ruled that the moment of birth had to be a good enough starting point.

He somewhat evaded the issue by writing: 'Conception is regarded as the natural beginning of life. But the moment of birth, though subordinate to the other, is endowed with a greater energy, since this energy is bought to bear on a complete human being and not a seed, and is added to a similar influence already brought to bear on the embryo . . .'

In his *Centrilocus* (a compressed version of the *Tetrabiblos*), Ptolemy collected the essence of his thoughts on astrology into a hundred sayings. Here are a few:

'Planets ruling the birth of tall people are in a position of elevation at the time of their horoscope. Those ruling short people are in declining houses.'

'Planets ruling the birth of thin people have no latitude, those of strong or fat people have a latitude.'

'Venus confers beauty and perfection to that part of the body indicated by the sign of the zodiac where she is situated.'

'When the moon is in the first quarter its humours will swell the body until the end of the second quarter, but when the moon passes into the two other quarters the humours will grow less and the body diminish.'

The Hermetic Tradition

One of the strange mystery cults to come out of Egypt was that of Hermes Trimegistus (or 'Thrice-greatest Hermes'). Although Hermes is a Greek name, the background to this religion does not seem to be purely Greek but has more to do with Thoth, the Egyptian counterpart of Hermes. Both deities are the patrons of medicine, so it is not surprising that the adherents of the Hermetic tradition practised medical astrology,

Page 38:
Jupiter with his two houses, Sagittarius and Pisces. The Greeks believed that the planets had a considerable influence on the signs they ruled. Miniature from 'De Sphaera', a fifteenth-century Italian manuscript. Biblioteca Estense, Modena.

Page 39:
A page from a fifteenth-century manuscript of Cicero's 'De Divinatione', written about 44 B.C., in which the sceptical Roman writer attacked all forms of divination and superstition. British Museum, London.

The signs of the zodiac painted on the lid of a sarcophagus of an Egyptian mummy. Nineteenth-century engraving.

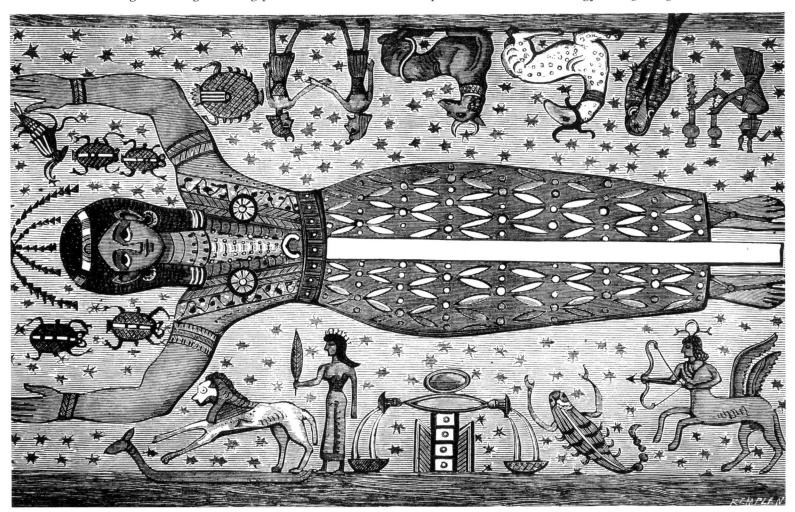

·IVPITER·

Benegno e ioue e de uirtu pianeta
Produce mathematici e doctori
Theologi er granfauij ne diueta
Alchuna gentil cosa o grandi honori :·

38

ETVS. OPINIO. EST. IAM. VSQVE AB. HE
roicis ducta temporibus eaq; & p. r. & omnium
gentium firmata consensu uersari quandam in
ter homines diuinationem quam graeci manti
cen appellant. id est presensionem & scientiam
rerum futurarum. magnifica quaedam res & salu
taris si modo est ulla. quaeq; proxima ad deorū
uum natura mortali possit accedere. Itaq; ut alia nos melius multa
q̃ graeci sic huic prestantissime rei nomen nostri a diuis graeci ut
plato interpretatur a furore duxerunt. Gentem quidem nullam ui
deo neq; tam humanam atq; doctam neq; tam imanem tamq; bar
baram quae non significari futura & a quibusdam intelligi prediciq;
posse censeat. Principio assirii ut ab ultimis auctoritatem repetam
propter planitiem magnitudinemq; regionum quas incolebant cū
caelum ex omni parte patens atq; apertum intuerentur traiectio
nes motusq; stellarum obseruauerunt. quibus notatis quid cuiq;
significaretur memoriae prodiderunt. qua in natione chaldei nō
ex artis sed ex gentis uocabulo nominati diuturna obseruatione si
derum scientiam putantur effecisse. ut predici poss& quid cuiq; cuē
turum & quo quisq; fato natus ess&. Eandem artem etiam egyptii lō
ginquitate temporum innumerabilibus pene seculis consecuti pu
tantur. Cilicum autem & pisidarum gentem & his finitima pamphi
lia quibus nationibus presuimus ipsi uolatibus auium cantibusq; cer
tissimis signis declarari res futuras putant. Quam uero graecia coloni
am misit in etholiam ioniam asiam siciliam italiam sine pytio aut

An Egyptian zodiac from the period of Roman rule.

further strengthening the bond between star-gazing and healing.

Hermetic literature had a very wide appeal and considerable influence. The number of books said to have been written under the name 'Hermes' was around 20,000. Now only seventeen or eighteen tantalizing fragments are known to exist. Certainly, the writings did not come from the hand of one Hermes, but from many who must have used the god's name to ensure a readership for their views on magic and healing. The mystery and obscurity surrounding this cult may very well have heightened its significance to the astrologers, magicians and alchemists of medieval times, who were entranced by Hermes Trimegistus and sought to penetrate his secrets.

The Hermetic tradition preached that man, the microcosm, is related to the universe, the macrocosm, as is demonstrated in the strange *Emerald Table*. This is a set of incomprehensible magical writings, believed originally to have been an emerald tablet inscribed with Phoenician characters which was discovered either by Sarah the Matriarch or Alexander the Great. The tablet was said to have been found in a tomb beside the remains of Hermes Trimegistus, who was traditionally not only the wisest of the wise but also Adam's grandson and the creator of the pyramids. Arabic and Latin versions of the writings have been found, all dating before or around the twelfth century. They are unintelligible, but from the viewpoint of magic and astrology this opening sentence is the key to the mysteries:

It is true, without falsehood, certain and very real,

That that which is on high is that which is below,

And that which is below is as that which is on high,

In order that the miracle of Unity may be very perpetual.

According to Hermes there are seven human types, corresponding to the seven planets, and the twelve signs of the zodiac govern different parts of the human body. This is the zodiacal man.

Hermes wrote: 'The macrocosm has animals, terrestrial and aquatic; in the same way man has fleas, lice and tapeworms. The macrocosm has rivers, springs and seas; man has intestines. The macrocosm contains breath—the winds—springing from its bosom; man has flatulence. The macrocosm has sun and moon; man has two eyes; the right related to the sun, the left to the moon. The macrocosm has twelve signs of the zodiac; man contains them too from his head, namely from the lion, to his feet, which correspond to the fish.'

This theory of correspondence probably goes back to the days of the pharaohs, but it became greatly elaborated by the Hermetic tradition.

Different ailments were assigned to the various signs of the zodiac, which were divided into three decanates of ten degrees each; e.g., stomach troubles belonged to the first decanate of Virgo, while lung troubles were found in the second decanate of Cancer.

Plants, herbs, and gems, and their relationships to particular stars all played a role in Hermetic magic and astrology. Magic incantations and talismans had long been used to obtain power and health, even before Hermetic lore became popular in Rome. Thus the cult of Hermes enlarged upon astrology, but it also linked it to the impossible (or implausible) realm of magic.

Rome

The Romans admired Greek ideas and practices, many of which they adopted. The Greek gods—and therefore the planets—were given Roman names. These are the ones we use today: Venus (Aphrodite); Mars (Ares); Jupiter (Zeus); Saturn (Kronos); Mercury (Hermes).

To begin with, the upper-class Romans looked down on astrology. They called horoscopes 'Babylonian numbers', and disparagingly dubbed the astrologers *Chaldei* ('Chaldeans'). Indeed, those who touted their astrological services among the ordinary folk and outside circuses were probably no more than itinerant fortune-tellers, ignorant of astronomy and astrology. Roman divination—much dependent upon augury and oracles—was in the hands of the

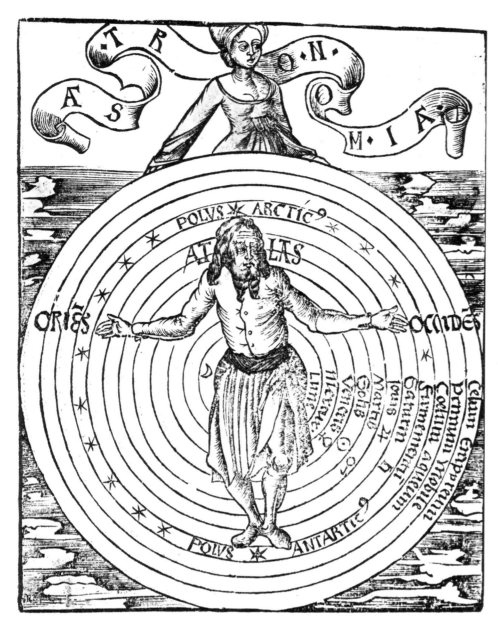

soothsayers, a powerful body who came from the top social group, and had a vested interest in keeping out the Chaldeans.

However, the large numbers of people of different races entering Rome and the state of uncertainty created by constant disorders helped astrology to gain a foothold among the intellectual upper classes as well as the masses. In 139 B.C. the soothsayers did manage to have the astrologers driven out of Rome and Italy, but this only made astrology more attractive, and its practitioners were consulted by letter, despite the decree of Cornelius Hispallus that declared 'the Chaldeans who exploit the people under the false pretext of consulting the stars'.

At the time of Julius Caesar's death in 44 B.C. a comet appeared in the heavens, and was the subject of dispute between soothsayers and astrologers. When Poseidonius, a man of great wisdom and intellect, sided with the astrologers (who claimed that the comet's appearance meant that Caesar had been placed among the stars) the intellectuals and the wealthy were won over to astrology.

However, there was still some learned opposition, and in his *De Divinatione* Cicero attacked all forms of divination: 'Superstition has usurped nearly everyone's wits and scored over human silliness.' Tersely he demanded of the astrologers: 'Were all those who perished at the battle of Cannae born under the same star?'

But such reasoned criticism did nothing to stem the tide. Astrology had become fashionable in Rome. By the first century A.D. the writings of a Roman poet, Marcus Manilius, show how firmly established was the belief in a relationship between the planets and the signs of the zodiac.

Man, the microcosm, and the universe, the macrocosm. Hermetic literature dealt with the correspondences between man and the universe. Woodcut from 'Margarita Philosophica' by Gregor Reisch (Basle, 1508). Royal Astronomical Society, London.

Opposite page:
Man reflects the heavens according to antique astrological concepts, since the zodiac and planets rule each part of the body. Page from 'Les très riches heures du Duc de Berry'. Fifteenth-century French manuscript. Musée Condé, Chantilly.

The Hermetic Cosmos.

42

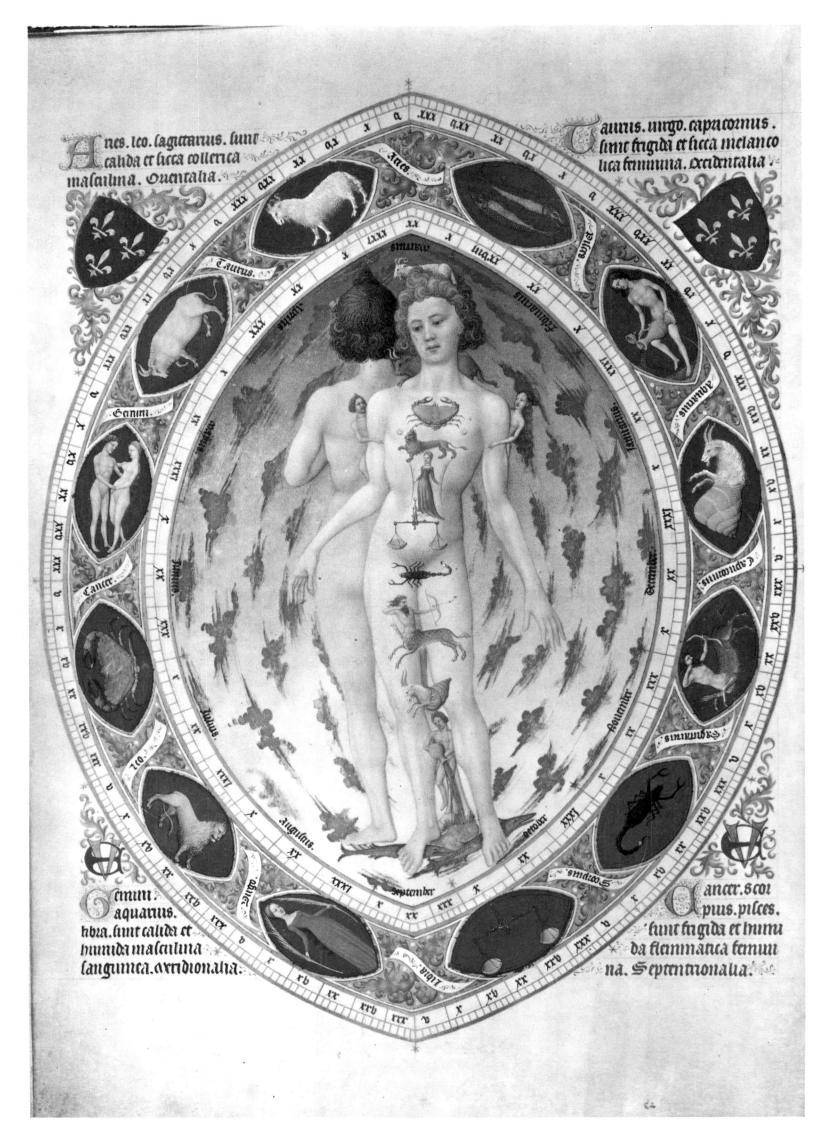

His poetry makes it clear how by this time it was accepted that the signs ruled various parts of the body:

The Ram defends the Head, the Neck, the Bull,
The Arms, bright Twins, are subject to your
 Rule:
I' th' Shoulders Leo, and the Crab's obeyed
I' th' Breast, and in the Guts the modest Maid:
I' th' Buttocks Libra, Scorpio warms Desires
In Secret Parts, and spreads unruly Fires:
The Thighs the Centaur, and the Goat
 commands
The Knees, and binds them up with double
 bands.
And Pisces gives Protection to the Feet.

The astrologers who practised in Rome were quite different from the Chaldeans of the streets. They were experts in numbers and geometrical forms, and they appealed very much to the rich and literate who needed more than the simple faith of the uneducated or pure philosophical debate.

Astrology affected the highest in the land. The emperor Augustus had, according to Suetonius, 'so much confidence in astrology that he made public his genethliac scheme, and struck silver coinage with the sign of Capricorn – the sign he had been born under.'

The strangely cruel emperor Tiberius also believed in astrology, although he must have had some reservations, since occasionally he had astrologers thrown from the high cliff on which stood his palace. However, one of their number, Thrasyllus became his intimate and was given the task of drawing up horoscopes for all the most important people in order that he could denounce them should their future appear liable to threaten the emperor's. Thus Tiberius could have them removed in good time. Domitian employed astrology in much the same way. But in A.D. 52 the emperor Claudius had the astrologers expelled from Rome.

When Nero came to power he brought back the astrologers. It is fascinating to read just how well established astrology was within Roman society in Nero's time in the *Satyricon* by Petronius. During an opulent banquet given by Trimalchio, an ostentatious (to say the least) 'self-made' man, a zodiacal triumph is served up for the edification of his guests.

This was a deep circular tray with the twelve signs of the zodiac around its edge. Over each of them the chef had placed some appropriate dainty, suggested by the subject. Over Aries, butter beans; over Taurus, beefsteak; over Gemini, testicles and kidneys; over Cancer, a garland (this was Trimalchio's own birth sign, and since he wanted to stay on good terms with his horoscope he avoided covering it with anything else); over the Lion, an African fig; over the Virgin, a young sow's udder; over Libra, the scales of balance with a tart in one pan and a cake in the other; over Scorpio, a lobster; over the Archer, a bullseye; over Capricorn, a horned fish (Capricorn was originally a goatfish, and not our simple goat); over Aquarius, a goose; and over Pisces, two mullets.

To display his doubtful erudition Trimalchio

holds forth on how he thinks the heavens affect people. Those born under the Ram would have lots of wool, herds, and a hard head. Under the sign are born most scholars and mutton heads. Since Trimalchio had been born under the Crab he had lots of legs to stand on. Under the Virgin are born effeminates, runaways, and candidates for the chain-gang; under Scorpio, poisoners and murderers; under the Fishes, fish-fryers and orators; and under the Scales, butchers and perfume-sellers, and anyone who weighs up things. Cross-eyed folk are born under Sagittarius.

In A.D. 77 Pliny the Elder wrote at the beginning of his *Natural History* that everyone wanted to know his own future and believed that the heavens showed clearly what was to be. Obviously, when a practice is so widespread there will be those who abuse it and take advantage of people's gullibility, and Pliny cites one Crinas of Marseilles 'who prescribed special diets for his clients based on the motions of the stars according to a mathematical formula, and who at his death left ten million sesterces . . .'

Some time later the poet Juvenal produced a satirical attack showing how astrology was demoralizing upper class Roman society. Women are particularly berated for consulting stargazers: *and will her lover outlive her? what greater boon could the gods bestow? Yet Tanaquil herself doesn't understand the darkening threat of Saturn or under what constellations Venus smiles, which months will be times of loss, and which of gain. But beware of meeting one whom you see clutching a worn calendar like a ball of clammy amber, one who doesn't inquire, but is herself inquired of; who, when her husband's travelling abroad or homing, won't go if Thrasyllus' 'Numbers' call her back. If she wants a drive to the first milestone, the book tells her the hour; if her rubbed eye itches, she checks her horoscope before she asks for a salve, and if she's ill abed, the hour for food is that prescribed for her by Petosiris . . .*

Yet, such amusing and telling assaults on people's blind faith in astrology had little effect, especially when Ptolemy's *Tetrabiblos* reached Rome.

As Rome declined in power, so the belief in astrology, and other occult sciences, reached manic proportions. In his *Science and Astrology* Michel Gauquelin suggests that this factor may well have contributed towards the political and moral degeneration of the Roman Empire.

Above left:
Cicero was one of the few learned Romans to deride astrology. 'If the state of the sky and the positions of the stars have so great an influence on all living things at their birth, it follows necessarily that this influence bears not only on humans, but also on animals. Can anything more absurd be said?' Statue. Museo Nazionale, Naples.

Above:
Petronius described the dishes at Trimalchio's ostentatious feast as symbolizing the zodiac, but the designer of this picture actually shaped the dishes after them. Engraving from an eighteenth-century Dutch edition of the 'Satyricon'.

Opposite, top:
Jupiter at the centre of the zodiac. Sculpture from the Villa Albani, Rome, c. second century A.D.

Opposite, bottom:
Roman zodiac signs engraved on an onyx.

The Chinese Tradition

No book on astrology can claim to be comprehensive unless it also looks at the patterns of development in areas which did not take their entire beginnings from Babylon and Greece. Not so surprisingly, stargazing in China was founded upon principles of astronomy and religious beliefs which differed from those of the West.

For most of us the China of today is nearly as mysterious as it was centuries ago. Although in the past astrology always played a significant role in Chinese life it is unlikely that the regime of Mao Tse Tung smiles on such old traditions—except in a disparaging way. When the Nationalist government was overthrown in 1949, the aged astrologers, who had already fallen out of favour through their link with and influence upon imperial power, either kept silent or went into miserable and penurious exile in Taiwan. Their influence was finally at an end, but they had had a very long and lucrative run.

Yet, outside China there are still millions of people of pure or mixed Chinese decent who, like their forebears, believe in a future moulded by the unseen forces which also rule the heavens. There are also those East Asian countries whose origins came very much under the influence of contemporary Chinese ideas.

For many oriental people, politics, business, and personal relationships are all guided by the signs in the sky, which, for the most part, are taken perfectly seriously. For instance, the last year of the Fire Horse, 1966 (which fortunately only occurs once every sixty years), prompted a lot of expectant Asian mothers to have abortions, since it is believed that any child born under this sign will bring misfortune to the family.

The Taoist and Buddhist religions incorporate astrological beliefs into their teachings, and therefore did much to foster and encourage such influences. A great Taoist author wrote: 'The Tao (or "Way") which is made manifest in the heavens by the sun is made manifest also in the hearts of men. It is the living force which brings existence into being. Here below it brings forth five varieties of cereal, and up above it ordains the movements of the stars.'

The western zodiac must have travelled along the early trade routes, but until the Jesuits reached Peking in 1601, and taught how it, as well as much other European knowledge could be applied, western astrology was basically foreign to the Chinese. They had a complex lore of their own, perhaps influenced by Indian ideas, and to a slight extent by Babylonian ones. Here are some astrological statements written around 100 B.C. but probably containing far older material, and they sound very much like those we already associate with Mesopotamia: 'When Mercury appears in company with Venus to the east, and when they are both red and shoot forth rays, then foreign kingdoms will be vanquished and the soldiers of China will be victorious.' 'If the moon is eclipsed near Ta-Chio (the name of a single star) this will bring hateful consequences to the Dispenser of Destinies.'

It is difficult to give accurate dates to the early development of Chinese astrology, partly because later commentators brought the ancient records up to date, correcting old ideas and adding new ones, and also because the 'Burning of the Books' in 213 B.C. must have destroyed a host of valuable early works. However, we do know that around 2000 B.C. the ancient Chinese worshipped the heavens and took note of their movements in order to regulate their agricultural society. Then, as now in China, the calendar was based upon the moon's cycle, and not like ours, upon the sun's. This calendar may have been adopted as early as 2637 B.C. In ancient times it was also firmly believed that the epochs of

A Chinese square cloth with writing on one side (1850) showing a chart with astrological symbols and explanations. MS OR 12221, British Museum, London.

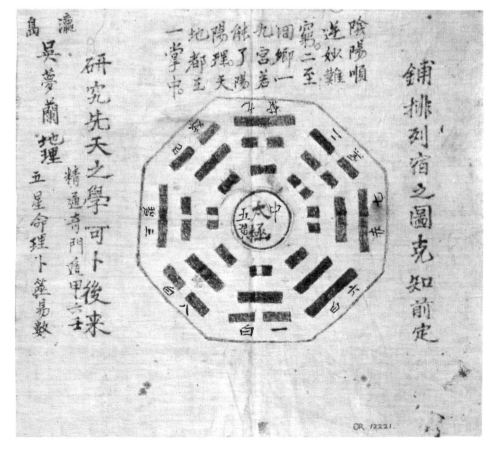

The Polos presenting letters to
the Grand Khan. We know
from the accounts of Marco
Polo's travels how powerful
was the influence of astrology
in the East in his time. From an
illuminated manuscript in the
Bodleian Library, Oxford.

For the Chinese the ox was
originally a star god, but his
stupidity forced him to remain
on earth to help the farmers
with the ploughing, but he
bore mankind no grudge.
Many—especially under
Indian influence—were
regarded as sacred animals.
Seventeenth-century jade,
Ming dynasty. Victoria and
Albert Museum, London.

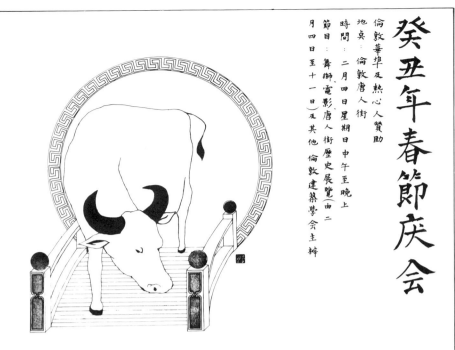

CHINESE NEW YEAR FESTIVAL 1973

SPONSORED BY THE GERRARD STREET CHINESE COMMUNITY
GERRARD STREET, W1. SUNDAY 4 FEBRUARY: NOON~EVENING.

Programme includes a Lion Dance Procession, Filmshows, an Exhibition (4-11 February), and other Sideshows.
Organised by the Architectural Association Festival Group

Koung-Tjee, ou Confucius

Among overseas Chinese communities belief in a future determined by the stars is widespread. This poster for a Chinese New Year Festival in London has the buffalo as its symbol (1973 was the last year of the buffalo). Poster designed by Keith Yeang.

The Chinese philosopher Confucius or K'ung Fu-tse, c. 551–478 B.C. As the founder of the system of cosmology, politics, and ethics known as Confucianism, he was more interested in reason than the supernatural, but he did not ignore important planetary predictions.

history were in some way related to the heavens.

The Chinese called their land the 'Middle Kingdom', and believed that it corresponded with the 'Middle Kingdom' in the skies where the stars never set. The emperor was called the 'Son of Heaven', and was thought to control the harmony between heaven and earth. The ruler, through his astrologer, knew the correct times of the seasons. Also vested in him was the knowledge which enabled him to predict and interpret the signs in the sky. If he failed to see such signs he had lost the favour of the unseen powers. Thus, it was essential for the emperor's advisers to watch and carefully calculate in order to provide accurate information, which obviously meant the astrologers played a very prominent role in society, since the credibility of the emperor in the eyes of his unsophisticated subjects was largely dependent upon their skills.

It has been suggested that the Hsia dynasty (1994–1523 B.C.) actually fell because the emperor's astrologers failed to predict an eclipse of the sun. Such an unheralded occurrence meant to the people that the heavens had turned against the reigning dynasty. In order to restore the balance between heaven and earth a new 'Son of Heaven' was chosen.

During the succeeding Shang dynasty the emperor was apparently obliged to identify closely with the seasons. At each he resided in a corresponding palace: in the spring the palace faced east; in the summer south; in the autumn west; and in the winter north. The emperor gave audience facing south because he represented the centre of the kingdom, which would be the Pole Star. The custom was probably instituted at a time when a particularly bright star had been observed close to the Pole. Describing the emperor's role, Confucius—that conservative promoter of the 'golden mean' in everything—said: 'One who governs the people by means of his virtue is like the Pole Star which keeps its place while the other stars circle it.'

This concept of the palaces was part of Chinese astronomy. The astrologers–astronomers did not watch the ecliptic, to which, in the first and second century A.D., they gave the name Yellow Road, but chose to observe the circumpolar stars since, weather permitting, these are visible all night the whole year round, unlike the ecliptic of which only half can be seen at any one time. The Middle Kingdom of the sky was divided into four palaces, namely Northern, Southern, Eastern, and Western. Chinese astronomers did not pay as much attention to the rising and setting of the stars as did their counterparts in Babylon, Egypt, and Greece. Instead they concentrated on the circumpolar constellations. There were twenty-eight of these, called asterisms, mansions or *hsui*, and they were located within the four palaces. They bear no relation to our zodiac, and may have arisen independently between 1000 and 800 B.C. or spread from India around that time, since Indian astrology also has twenty-eight *nakshatras* or mansions, although the two sets of names are totally different. The fact that there are twenty-eight may well arise from a rough estimate of the moon's monthly course through the mansions. Five of these

constellations seem purely Chinese, seventeen are shared with India, and eighteen with Arabia. Curiously enough, many constellations known to Babylon and Greece were not recorded by the Chinese and vice versa.

In the Northern Palace are Gryphon, Ox, Bat, Rat, Swallow, Bear, and Porcupine. In the Southern Palace are Tapir, Sheep, Mutjak, Horse, Deer, Serpent, and Worm. In the Eastern Palace are Hornless Dragon, Dragon, Badger, Hare, Tiger, and Leopard. In the Western Palace are Wolf, Dog, Pheasant, Raven, Monkey, Ape, and Cock.

To complicate matters further some of these animals also appear in what we can term the oriental zodiac. Not only do these creatures give their names to the twelve months, but also to the divisions of the hour circle, and later to the twelve-year cycle. This circle of animals seems to have been imported around 300 or 400 B.C., although some historians put it as early as 500 B.C.

Nobody is quite sure precisely how the circle of beasts came into being, but there is a legend that Buddha invited all the animals in creation to meet him one New Year with the promise of a present if they attended. Only twelve turned up, so to each he gave a year. The Rat or Mouse (this

may stand first because for the ancient Chinese a new day started at midnight – the hour when rats are at their most active); the Buffalo, Ox, or, in Thailand, Cow; the Tiger (Panther in Mongolia); the Cat (Hare or Rabbit in Thailand); the Dragon (in Thailand the Great Dragon, in Persia the Crocodile); the Snake or Serpent (in Thailand small Dragon); the Horse; the Sheep or Goat; the Monkey; the Cock or Hen; the Dog; the Boar or Pig. Every sixty years instead of the ordinary horse the Fire Horse reigns. So, if one were to ask an Asian for his or her birth sign he or she would tell you the year of one of the above animals.

A deeper insight into the significance of these animals can be found in a Buddhist text: 'When the twelve animals have accomplished their meritorious work, they make a solemn vow in the presence of all the Buddhas to see to it that night and day there shall always be one of them travelling, preaching, and converting, while the other eleven remain quietly practising goodness. The Rat begins on the first day of the seventh moon, and converts all beings who have the form of rats. He persuades them to give up evil actions and exhorts them to do good. The others in succession do the same and when the thirteenth day comes the Rat begins again. In

Tigers were honoured as the emblems of the West, the direction of Kun-lun and the Western Paradise. They were also feared, since the Chinese believed if a tiger ate a man his soul became the beast's slave and preyed upon other men. Painting by Chen Chu-chung. British Museum, London.

50

the same way they go on until the end of the twelve months, and the twelve years, with a view to bringing all living beings under the Rule. It is for this reason there are so many meritorious actions upon the earth, since even the animals preach and convert, teaching the unsurpassable doctrine of the Buddha.'

Records from about 200 B.C. show the duties and importance of the imperial astrologer: 'This exalted gentleman must concern himself with the stars in the heavens, keeping a record of the changes and movements of the planets, the sun and the moon, in order to examine the movements of the terrestrial world with the object of prognosticating good and bad fortune. He divides the territories of the nine regions of

Detail of emperor's marriage robe, showing clawed imperial dragon, a rain spirit symbolizing the emperor himself, and three of the twelve imperial symbols. Above, the constellations, to which the emperor made offerings at the Altar of Heaven; left, the 'fu' symbol of happiness; right, the axe symbolizing the power to punish. Nineteenth century. Victoria and Albert Museum, London.

Far left:
Chinese pottery tomb figures representing the cardinal points. Above: woman seated on the White Tiger of the West. Below: woman riding the Sombre Warrior (tortoise and snake) of the North. Six Dynasties Period (A.D. 220–589). William Rockhill Nelson Gallery, Kansas City, Missouri.

Left:
Chinese pottery tomb figures representing the cardinal points. Above: woman riding the Green Dragon of the East. Below: woman riding the Red Bird of the South. Six Dynasties period (A.D. 220–589). William Rockhill Nelson Gallery, Kansas City, Missouri.

Top: animals of the Chinese zodiac stamped on to a talisman. Below: a Chinese medallion showing a square world and the Great Bear constellation.

the empire in accordance with their dependence on particular celestial bodies. All the fiefs and principalities are connected with the stars and from this their prosperity or misfortune could be ascertained. He makes prognostications according to the twelve years of the Jupiter cycle of good and evil of the terrestrial world. From the colours of the five kinds of clouds he determines the coming of floods or drought, abundance or famine. From the twelve winds he draws conclusions about the state of harmony of heaven and earth and takes note of good and bad signs that results from their accord or disaccord. In general he concerns himself with five kinds of phenomena so as to warn the emperor to come to the aid of the government and to allow for variations in the ceremonies according to the circumstances.'

The brothers Sho and Shi—who may only have been legendary imperial astrologers—did not seem to be adept in their craft, for they were beheaded for a failure to foresee and prevent an eclipse.

However, ancient Chinese astronomers made some surprisingly accurate observations, especially of comets which they believed to emanate from each of the planets. In 444 B.C. they calculated the year to be $365\frac{1}{4}$ days and they were the first to see Halley's Comet in 240 B.C. Sun-spots, which were not written about until the time of Galileo, were regularly noted from 28 B.C. by the Chinese, who related them to the quality of the harvest. The planets were given elements and directions: Jupiter, wood, east; Mars, fire, south; Saturn, earth, centre; Venus,

Buddha seated on a dragon. Buddhism did much to spread the influence of astrology in China. Watercolour of the seventeenth or eighteenth-century. Religionskundliche Sammlung der Universitat Marburg.

metal, west; Mercury, water, north. The Chinese seem to have been the only people to use wood as one of the basic elements.

The regulation of the calendar and its publication were the responsibility of the government, which shows just how important was this table of days—not only for the apportionment of agricultural tasks, the collection of taxes and the administration of justice, but also for providing the majority of people with a guide as to how they might successfully avoid thwarting the harmony of the world and running contrary to the designs of the unseen powers.

Originally, the days were arranged in groups of sixty, but then, in order to regulate the seasonal duties to the movements of the earth and moon, the calendar was made up of alternating long (thirty days) and short (twenty-nine days) months. Usually, there were twelve to a year, but in order to keep the calendar in close relation to the rotation of the earth an extra-or intercalary—month was added every thirty-two or thirty-three months, which meant that every third year or so the calendar, as provided by the astrologers, stated there would be thirteen months to that particular year.

In 104 B.C. the renowned grand astrologer and archivist, Ssu-ma Ch'ien, together with others, set out the reforms to the calendar: 'Thereupon they determined the points east and west, set up sundials and gnomons, and contrived water clocks. With such means they marked out the twenty-eight mansions according to their positions at various points in the four quarters, fixing the first and last days of each month, the equinoxes and solstices, the movements and relative positions of the heavenly bodies and the phases of the moon.' The four seasons began with the new moon of the first, fourth, seventh, and tenth months, and the second, fifth, eighth, and eleventh moons contained equinoxes and solstices. Until 1927 this remained the official calendar, and is still used, albeit unofficially.

The modern Asian calendar differs from ours because of the date of the New Year. As a result of the moon's somewhat erratic cycle the oriental new year starts a little later than our regular 1st January, and may be in January or February. Thus, anyone born in either of these months who wanted to work out his birth sign according to the Chinese zodiac might have some difficulty in finding out whether his birth date fell just in an old or a new year. Another difference is that the Sino-Vietnamese calendar is calculated in sixty-year cycles, and is now in its seventy-seventh year cycle. This began in 1924, and will end—inauspiciously enough for the western mind—in 1984! This sixty-year period is also divided into six ten-yearly cycles, and every second or third year has an intercalary month.

Anyone born on the first day of the Asian year is said to have the characteristics most predominant for that particular year, and will stand the best chance of achieving success. Popular belief holds that whatever you do this first day will be repeated through the year, so you are advised to enjoy yourself and avoid quarrels, creditors, the police, and hard work.

In eastern countries New Year's Day is a very important celebration, and all kinds of fireworks are exploded to frighten away the evil spirits.

Ancient Chinese scientists showed a preference for reason rather than belief in unseen occult forces. In the first centuries of the Christian era they designed a primitive seismograph, measured the obliquity of the ecliptic, and calculated the moon's elliptical orbit almost correctly. But such discoveries did not stem the tide of superstitious beliefs in invisible powers, which must be propitiated, and whose numbers were vastly increased by political and social upheavals.

Wang Ch'ung (A.D. 27–100) was an enlightened and rational critic of his times. He wrote: 'On average there is about one lunar eclipse in about 180 days, and a solar eclipse in about every 41 or 42 months. Eclipses are regular occurrences and are not caused by political action. All anomalies and catastrophes are of the same class, and are never dependent upon political events.' He pointed out that earthquakes, comets and suchlike were not sent by the spirits to warn the emperor of their displeasure but were caused naturally. He did not dispute that man was prey to destiny, but did not think that fate could be manipulated by magic or symbolic ceremonies. Wang Ch'ung seemed to subscribe to the belief in personal astrology, which was growing in his time, and apparently felt that man's will could achieve little in the face of strictly predetermined fate.

His commonsense attitude to natural disasters was not shared by a certain Wei Chui who, in the sixth century A.D., attributed catastrophes to various creatures. Disasters happened whenever a monster was born on earth or some miraculous creature appeared in the heavens. Thus: a two-headed calf foretold the destruction of the temple of the ancestors; a horse in the sky meant war; and a cock with horns predicted royal prerogative being overthrown by a minor official. Worst of all were the Calamities of the Pig: 'Of all the signs of evil augury, these are much the most common; they signify that a person holding public office is perverse'.

Wang Ch'ung's scepticism suggested an independence and choice which few cared to adopt. Indeed, the imperial establishment depended upon people believing devoutly that mysterious powers controlled the emperor's fortune. Such concepts could be skilfully manipulated to obtain obedience from a credulous people: the past could be explained in terms of the influence of these occult powers, and the present might be moulded to suit the prediction of their operations in the future. All in all, astrology was a valuable tool with which to control men's lives, giving astrologers and priests a power which could not easily be upset, lest the unseen wreak vengeance.

Taoist magicians of the first centuries A.D. believed that every part of the body contained gods who were also rulers of heaven, earth, stars, mountains and waters. Once again, here is the concept of the macrocosm and microcosm. By meditation an individual might commune with these deities, and obtain from them moral teachings for his health and welfare. Correct

Peking Observatory was built at the end of the thirteenth century, during the Mongol dynasty. The instrument in the foreground showing four dragons chained to the earth and upholding the spheres is cast in solid bronze.

54

An example of an Oriental horoscope.

Opposite, top:
Oriental zodiac. In the East the zodiac was adapted from the Western concept.

Opposite, bottom:
The Japanese fortune-teller or 'uranaisha' is very popular with ordinary people. Besides divining the future these fortune-tellers exorcize demons and create charms to ward off all types of evil.

ascendant at any particular time. Popular astrology was often of a fairly primitive nature, as found in the Fen-Chui ('Wind and Water') Almanac. This was a simple mixture of astrology and magic-science for the countryman, showing how to trace the paths of sun and moon among the twenty-eight mansions, and their influence on the body and the colours of nature. A planet was beneficial if it showed bright and clear, but malefic if dim and 'wounded'.

The imperial almanac, published annually, swayed the lives of innumerable Chinese over the ages. It gave specialized and detailed predictions for that particular year as well as for each sign in relation to the ruling year, and included long-range weather forecasts and rituals for placating the spirits. It also contained lists of forbidden things to do that year – such as marriages between certain signs (the Tiger must not marry with a Buffalo, or the Horse wed a Rat), and there were also recipes for medicines and food. This almanac must have caused a good deal of heartsearching and misery. How many promising careers or romances were nipped in the bud! But it demonstrates the kind of power the authorities could wield over anything from matrimony to politics in a society conditioned to accept astrological prognostications.

We gain further insight on the influence of astrologers in the thirteenth century when Marco Polo visited China. He wrote that in the city of Kanbalu there were 5000 astrologers and soothsayers supported by the emperor. They used astrolabes, and made meteorological forecasts as well as predicting epidemics, wars, and plots against the government. Nobody made a journey without first consulting these savants, who would not dream of giving advice until they knew the year, month, day, and hour of an individual's birth.

Marco Polo also recounted how no funeral could be held among the upper classes until the date was approved by an astrologer. A corpse's natal chart had to be checked to calculate a suitable day for its cremation! Sometimes we might suspect these astrologers of being malicious simply in order to show off their authority. A family could wait up to six months for the 'right' funeral day, which, not surprisingly, necessitated very heavy coffins, preservatives, and sweet-smelling spices. Even on the appointed day the astrologer's whim might still be exercised, for he could order the body to be removed from the house in a certain direction, so requiring a hole to be bored through a wall!

The astrologers flourished for many centuries. Although supported by the imperial court, they preferred to remain independent. In this way, individuals could employ their skills to further their own ideas and interests. Symbolism neatly cloaked such practices. If a suggestion failed or a prediction went awry, this symbolism provided useful camouflage or, alternatively, the astrologers could intimate that their messages had been wrongly interpreted by the officials.

During the Tai Ping Rebellion in the mid-nineteenth century, astrologers helped plan military campaigns, and in the early years of the Republic the warlords made use of their advice

breathing, careful diet, the influence of sun and moonlight could all contribute to purifying the body so that it might rise to heaven where body and soul would gain immortality. These theories are obviously the very antithesis of Wang Ch'ung's philosophy that man's health and prosperity were not dependent upon his moral qualities or conduct.

Originally horoscopes were concerned only with the emperor and his country, and only later did the personal horoscope become popular. Ancient Chinese prediction was based upon: the moon's altitude and conjunction to planets, and fixed stars; the sun, its position and colour; and the rising and setting and conjunction of the planets and their relationships to fixed stars. The astrologers did not pay particular attention to which star or constellation was in the about manoeuvres and troop movements. The Empress Tzu Hsi, who ruled China during the Boxer Rebellion, owed her vagaries in policy to the counsel of the imperial astrologers. In her own lifetime she arranged her burial place to conform with their dictates, although this entailed moving the remains of some royal ancestress, and when her funeral took place at 5 a.m. on 27th November, 1909, it was at the time appointed by the astrologers.

After the declaration of the Republic in 1912 the majority of astrologers either abandoned their careers or turned into simple fortune-tellers. Since astrology was associated with dynastic regimes, the new government was not inclined to view it sympathetically.

The Japanese Tradition

Before we leave China let us take a brief glance at Japan, where ancient astrology borrowed much of its lore from Indian and Chinese sources. In the millennium before Christ the royal court was interested in interpreting the future in terms of the movements of the celestial bodies, and this interest was increased by the arrival of Buddhism. Certain Japanese emperors, generals, and admirals used astrology to predict political policies, the weather, and also to plan military and naval campaigns.

The popularity of astrology rose and fell over the ages, but in an attempt to make his country face the exigencies of the twentieth century the Emperor Meiji (1867–1912) tried to discourage such practices. Strangely enough, in 1922 the head of Kyoto's Astronomical Observatory, Kumamoto Arihasa, published a translation and adaptation of Raphael (an early nineteenth-century English astrologer) and, because of the astronomer's eminence, the book was received seriously.

Since the Second World War there has been a revival of Japanese interest in astrology. At present, there are estimated to be around 200,000 members of a Japanese federation which includes astrologers, clairvoyants, and graphologists. One teacher of the subject, Youko Shiojima, who gives tuition personally, or by correspondence course, will only accept university graduates as students. He has trained more than thirty who practise in major Japanese cities and small towns.

The Japanese no longer calculate the beginning of their year from the moon, which means that their year, like ours, starts on 1st January, although they do use the oriental animal zodiac. At the really popular level the pavement astrologers or *Ekisha* do a roaring trade. At night, clad in traditional black kimonos, they set up stalls in doorways where they work until the small hours, attracting the attention of passers-by. Their methods of prediction are a mixture of basic astrology and palmistry with a neat little escape clause. They use the customer's date and hour of birth, and check predictions arising from this against the lines on the hand. To discover just how likely the forecast will be special sticks are shaken in a container, some removed, and the rest counted. Accuracy is said to rest on the numbers remaining.

India and Mexico

Opposite page:
The coronation of King Birendra Bir Bikram of Nepal in 1975 which took place according to the dictates of Brahmin astrological traditions.

India

When the last of the Hindu kings, Birendra Bir Bikram Shah Dev of Nepal was crowned at precisely 8.37 a.m. on 24th February, 1975, it was because the court astrologers deemed this to be the most propitious time for the young king and his country. These influential men come from the topmost Hindu caste, the Brahmins, who are priests and scholars. It had taken them three years to elect a suitable moment for his coronation. During the first the king was in mourning for his father, and the second, the year 2030 by the Katmandu calendar, was considered less than fortunate since it ended in a zero. Despite a modern education at Eton and Harvard the king upheld the traditions that most Hindus and non-Hindus of that part of the world take very seriously. Astrology governs almost every aspect of daily life among both the humble and the educated, and there has been an attempt to reintroduce its study into Indian universities.

Although Jawaharlal Nehru, India's first prime minister, tried to discourage the use of astrology in attempts to modernize his country, nonetheless in a letter to his sister about the birth of his first grandson in 1944, he wrote: 'In my letter to Indu I suggested to her to ask you to get a proper horoscope made by a competent person. Such permanent records of the date and time of birth are desirable. As for the time I suppose the proper solar time should be mentioned and not the artificial time which is being used outside now. War time is at least an hour ahead of the normal time.'

Predictions based on the movements of the heavenly bodies have been among Indian customs for many centuries. However, astrology in the subcontinent is not as ancient as was originally supposed, although Indian astrologers claim that the West has taken much of its lore from theirs. In very early times other forms of divination, such as dream interpretation and collecting omens, were preferred to astrology, but by the period of the Gupta dynasty (fourth century A.D.) reading the stars held pride of place, and remains too deeply embedded in religion and the structure of Indian society simply to be cast aside because man can now travel to the moon.

Not much is known about ancient Indian astronomy, but it may well have been influenced to some extent by Mesopotamia. The *Rig-Veda*,

This masked dog from Mexico may symbolize Xolotl, the god of death and brother of Quetzacoatl, disguised to accompany the dead to the world of the after-life. The dog also featured prominently in the Aztec divinatory calendar. National Museum of Anthropology, Mexico City.

the oldest of the sacred Hindu books, charted the heavens with twenty-seven mansions (star groupings) or *nakshatras*. These were subsequently made up to twenty-eight, and probably influenced contemporary Chinese, and later Arabian astronomy. After the establishment of Alexandria, Greek theories on astronomy and astrology filtered into India, bringing the twelve signs of the zodiac, and the seven-day week. Originally, India seems to have had two sets of names for the zodiac: one was the Sanskrit spelling of the Greek words before their meanings were understood, and the other the actual translation, thus: Ram or Goat, Bull, Couple (Man and Wife), Crab, Lion, Virgin, Balance, Scorpion or Bee, Bow, Sea-Monster or Antelope, Pot, and Fish. Incidentally, Hindus call the arcs of thirty degrees in any circle by the twelve signs.

India made good use of the new knowledge, and embellished it with her own skilful mathematics. Eventually, this elaborated astrology, and the mathematics, passed back to Europe by the way of the Arabs.

In *The Origin of the Zodiac* Rupert Gleadow points out that some modern Indian astrologers may use one of two sorts of zodiac: the tropical or moving one, called *sayana* (measured from the tropics), and several fixed or sidereal versions called *nirayana* (marked by the constellations). Because the original reference star has been lost over the centuries, the astrologers try to calculate the actual difference – the *ayanamsha* – between the two. Thus, when Indian astrologers forecast the end of the world for the 5th

February, 1962 – the most momentous kind of mundane astrology – a British astrologer, Edward Whitman, was able to write in the *Sunday Times* of 4th February that he was not overly worried by this prediction since the Hindus had used a fixed zodiac whereas he and other western astrologers employed the moving one. Whether that explains why the world did not come to an end on the following day, or what would have been proved if it had, this writer must leave to the reader.

Although some educated Indians criticize astrology because it interferes with almost every aspect of daily life, it is in fact unusual not to seek the advice of astrologers. From before birth until after death Hindus and non-Hindus alike seek the guidance of their stars.

While the wealthy will regularly consult a scholarly astrologer, in much the same way a private patient might use his doctor (even calling him in when someone is unwell to determine if the illness will last long enough to make it worthwhile sending for the doctor), the poor will go to the street-corner astrologer whenever something arises that seems to require specialized prognostication.

Private houses and public buildings are erected in consultation with astrologers. Journeys and moving house are undertaken only on astrologically fortunate days. Even medicine has help from the heavens: operations are performed on days beneficial to the patient, although an unlucky day for the surgeon might prove equally inauspicious for the patient. It has even been mooted quite seriously that in

hospitals the patient's horoscope should be displayed at the foot of the bed alongside the usual progress chart. Indian astrologers have also produced some outstandingly successful mundane predictions: the outbreak of the First World War, the Second World War, and the defeat of Hitler.

A fundamental difference between Indian and western astrology is that the former is closely allied to the religion and philosophy which structure society. Most astrologers come from the Brahmin or priestly caste, and so their art is generally regarded as divine. Astrology is one of the six *angas*–aids to understanding the sacred Vedic texts. Many Indians adhere to the concepts of caste, reincarnation, and karma. This last is the principle of ethical causation, by which the effects of all human actions must be fully worked out in the present or some future existence. It applies as much to groups and nations as individuals and is the foundation of Hindu and Buddhist philosophy. Many westerners see karma as pure fatalism, but astrology is reckoned to give the human being a choice, and a chance of salvation: for the karma may be influenced by following the clues to be found in the horoscope–which demonstrates that the belief is not one of total submission to an inevitable fate.

Indian astrology regards the cosmos–particularly the sun and planets–as working with the individual in developing character and understanding of self in an effort to achieve release from all that is base. The Indian looks into the horoscope to find out what would bring him the best on earth and in heaven, for the birth chart describes the general tendencies in the individual's life. Some western psychologists have suggested that Indians actually consult their horoscopes to find out their real desires, and this theory could apply equally to non-Indians who rely heavily on the advice of astrologers. A man's character and immediate future are thought to be caused by his own deeds in a past life, and while he may have to endure events which have already begun, the horoscope can provide a key to the hidden factors in his character which could counteract future misfortune. Thus, astrology for the Indian is not only an indication of what is to come, but also a help in improving some future existence.

Naturally, astrology plays a significant part in Indian marriage, sexual relations and birth. If we decided to have an arranged marriage we would think it essential to see a photograph of our potential partner for life; an Indian would be more anxious to examine a horoscope of his prospective bride. Advertisements for marriage partners in the personal columns of daily papers give the usual details of appearance, chastity, financial position, caste, and also the signs under which any interested party should have been born. Horoscopes are offered and sought as a foundation for opening matrimonial negotiations. Unless the horoscopes complement each other the possibility of marriage is ruled out. However, astrologers are human, and financial inducements may very effectively be used to persuade them to alter relevant birth charts if hearts

Pyramid of the Sun at Teotihuacán, Mexico, which was dedicated to the 'plumed serpent' Quetzalcoatl and the rain-god Thaloc.

The Stone of the Sun or Aztec calendar stone. This piece of olivine basalt weighs 25.5 metric tons. It was made by the Aztecs in the fifteenth century, and the reliefs show the sun-god Tonatiuh or 'earthquake'. The four rectangles around him contain the four previous suns, named 'wind', 'tiger', 'rain', and 'water'. The Aztecs believed that they were living in the age of the fifth sun which would destroy humanity. National Museum of Anthropology, Mexico City.

Illustration from the Jamnapattra of Prince Navanibal Singh of Lahore showing Aries. This magnificent book contains a great deal of general astrological information. Sanskrit MS OR 5259. British Museum, London.

dictate romance and the stars suggest otherwise.

Astrologers believe the horoscope will show the basic characters of bride and groom, of which they allow three types: *deva* ('divine'), *manusha* ('human') and *rakshasa* ('diabolical'). It seems unlikely that a divine or a human type will be permitted to marry a diabolical one, although this is to some extent dependent upon the sex of the types.

What else does the astrologer seek to learn from the horoscopes? Potential sexual appetites can be determined, and, while not necessarily preventing a marriage, are worth serious consideration. Not only is sexual harmony between the partners divined but also physical, mental, and temperamental compatibility. Other important considerations are: long life, hereditary illnesses, possible promiscuity, and whether or not either partner will bring good fortune to the other and also to the two familes. Once the horoscopes have been examined and agreed, the astrologers fix the wedding date, but there are certain specified times when no marriages may take place.

A couple must attempt to conceive a child at the time appointed by the astrologer. Saturday, Tuesday, the fourth, eighth, ninth, and fourteenth days of the moon's cycle are unsuitable for conceptions, as are new and full moons. Once a woman is pregnant she may determine the sex of her child by performing certain rituals at astrologically specified times. Astrology sets the date for naming the baby, and the initial of its name is the result of computations involving the stars under which the child is born. A youngster is guided by the astrologer in anything from the time of its first haircut to the start of education.

Another curious aspect of Indian astrology is

An Indian zodiac. It should be read anti-clockwise from the top left-hand corner.

Despite its obvious Eastern flavour most of the signs in this Indian zodiac are quite familiar to Western eyes.

all kinds of personal revelations about birth, education, career, marriage, homes, and illness, and even details of parental background.

The sceptical may smile and dub the *Nadi Granthas* as fairground chicanery – no different from those weighing machines which trot out 'you will meet a tall, dark, handsome stranger and cross water', along with your weight, but plenty of western people, who have been intrigued enough to have their future read by this method, have been startled by the accuracy of the revelations and predictions.

Mexico

The mighty Aztec empire that fell before the force of the Spanish Conquistadors in the early sixteenth century had inherited the religions and practices of previous civilizations which had inhabited that part of Central America. Like them, this incredibly short-lived but highly complex society had an obsession with measuring the passage of time. By the use of certain fixed stars calendars were evolved to mark the movements of the sun, moon, and planets, and to appoint the seasons, and also the times for performing the rites associated with each month. The Aztecs believed every person's fate on earth, mode of death, and existence beyond the grave was dictated by the sign under which he or she was born. Thus, it was the belief in omens and inexplicable phenomena which had the greatest power upon the life and thought of these early Mexicans.

The *tonalpouhque*, or soothsayers, were a category of priests trained to understand the lore of the *tonalpoualli* – the divinatory calendars – which were one of the foundations of higher learning. Once qualified, the soothsayers did not enter a temple, but pursued their profession among the people. Since the rituals attending birth, baptism, and marriage, or the times of a journey or military campaign might not be undertaken without reference to the highly complicated divinatory calendars, these priests were kept very busy, and their advice was paid for with food, clothing, and meals.

The Aztecs were filled with noble pessimism. From our viewpoint such pessimism was justified, but the nobility sprang from their struggle to survive and live while feeling themselves to be the hapless victims of unseen forces. They were not defeatists, and in one sense were imbued with a glorious certainty of resurrection. From observing nature the Aztecs concluded that neither it nor mankind dies forever, for although the sun is vanquished each evening it rises again on the morrow.

Comets, earthquakes, and other phenomena were carefully recorded, and most of these were considered to be unfavourable omens. When a great light appeared streaming from earth heavenwards in 1509 (probably zodiacal light), this was later assumed to have predicted the coming of the Spaniards. The Aztec enthusiasm for collecting omens meant they kept copious records in their hieroglyphic style of writing. The Spaniards, who did not share their new captives' tolerance for other gods and customs, destroyed many of these works on the grounds

the *Nadi Granthas*. These palm-leaf manuscripts, containing countless ready-made horoscopes, are said to be very ancient – one is reputed to be the work of an astrologer in 30 B.C. The *Nadi* adherents explain that there are 3600 basic types of fate in any day: 150 rise over the horizon during one hour. Using the existing horoscope chosen according to the client's time of birth, or sometimes his or her palm print, the astrologer – usually of the street-booth variety – will make that they were about black magic. Fortunately for later historians some survived. From these, and the conquerors' and colonizers' own accounts a picture of Aztec cosmology emerges which, while quite different from anything we have already examined, clearly demonstrates that the Aztecs were prey to many of the hopes and fears shared by those who lived in other lands and at other times.

The Aztec divinatory calendar, like those of other Mexican civilizations, was based upon thirteen numbers (1–13), and twenty names and their signs. Here are the translations: crocodile or water monster, wind, house, lizard, snake, death, deer, rabbit, water, dog, monkey, dead grass, reed, ocelot, eagle, vulture, earthquake, flint, rain, flower. The divinatory year was of 260 days (13×20), and began at 1 crocodile and finished on 13 flower. It was divided into twenty sections of thirteen, each starting with number 1 and a different sign. Every group was regarded as lucky, unlucky or nondescript depending on its first day. Since other numbers and signs, and their combination, might also be fortunate, unfortunate, or indifferent, prediction was no simple task: in fact, there were probably 260 different kinds of fortune! Numbers containing seven, and ten and above were usually beneficial, while anything with nine was just the opposite.

Each section was under the dominion of one or two gods: the sun, moon, Venus, and other deities. The four cardinal points controlled five signs respectively. The compass points also ruled the day and the year in this order: east, north, west, and south. Thus, the day and year had qualities attributed to each quarter: the east was equated with fruitfulness, the north with sterility, the west with decline, age and demise, and the south had a nondescript quality. In the same order the cardinal points also governed the groups of thirteen.

While they obviously felt there was no way of placating inexorable destiny some juggling with fate was attempted. If a child was born under an unlucky sign, up to four days in that particular section were allowed to elapse in order that it could be named under a more favourable sign.

Those born under the group 1 ocelot were doomed to perish as captives; 2 rabbit produced topers; 4 dog gave great riches; 4 wind was good for magicians; 1 house favoured doctors; and 7 flower benefited artists and weavers. Marriages could not go ahead until the soothsayers had examined the signs under which the couple were born. Suitable wedding days were reed, monkey, crocodile, eagle, and house.

The solar and divinatory calendars were quite different, which meant one day might be named in two separate ways. The 365-day solar year was divided into 18 months of 20 days each, and the 5 'hollow' days were thought of as particularly unlucky. Each month was called after some seasonal event or the ceremonies celebrated during it. The year itself was named after its first day. Since this name came from the divinatory calendar it decided whether or not a particular year would be fortunate. Because of

mathematical calculations only four names were possible: reed, flint, house, and rabbit, and 1 reed was certainly unfavourable. By our calendar this was 1519–the year of the European invasion.

The Aztecs particularly revered Venus, and its god was Quetzalcoatl ('Plumed Serpent')–the priests' god, the patron of self-sacrifice, the calendar, learning, penance, and culture. Because of the planet's appearance in both morning

Xochipieti, the Mexican god of joy, music, dancing, vegetation, and fruitfulness, was also the bestower of punishments for various kinds of misdeeds.

Quetzalcoatl, the Aztecs' patron of the calendar, wisdom, culture and self-sacrifice, was associated with the much-revered planet Venus. Museum voor Volkerkunde, Holland.

and evening it was the symbol of life and death. From their own – and previous societies' – observations, the Aztecs noted that 5 Venus years equal 8 sun years. These cycles only converged after 65 sun and 104 Venus years. The number 104 is the longest period in Mexican time-keeping, and was called one 'old age', for it was composed of two 'centuries'. The Mexican 'century' of 52 years was symbolized by a bunch of stalks tied together. Every 52 years the Aztecs feared that the century's final sunset would indeed be the last forever. To repel the ever-threatening and terrible forces of darkness and the void the priests performed the rite of 'binding the years' by sacrificing a human captive, and lighting a torch which was plunged into the victim's

wound. Thus fire was rekindled with blood, and the sun would rise once more. The world had escaped destruction for another 'century'.

Other places

We are far away in time and distance, and might profitably use the rest of this chapter to glance at how other distant places regard astrology, but to do this let us return to our own century.

Obviously, immigration and colonization have meant that particular countries and continents are under the aegis of different astrological traditions. Some borrow from Europe, some from China, and some from India. It has even been suggested that Mexican astrology may have been influenced by ancient Chinese lore travelling

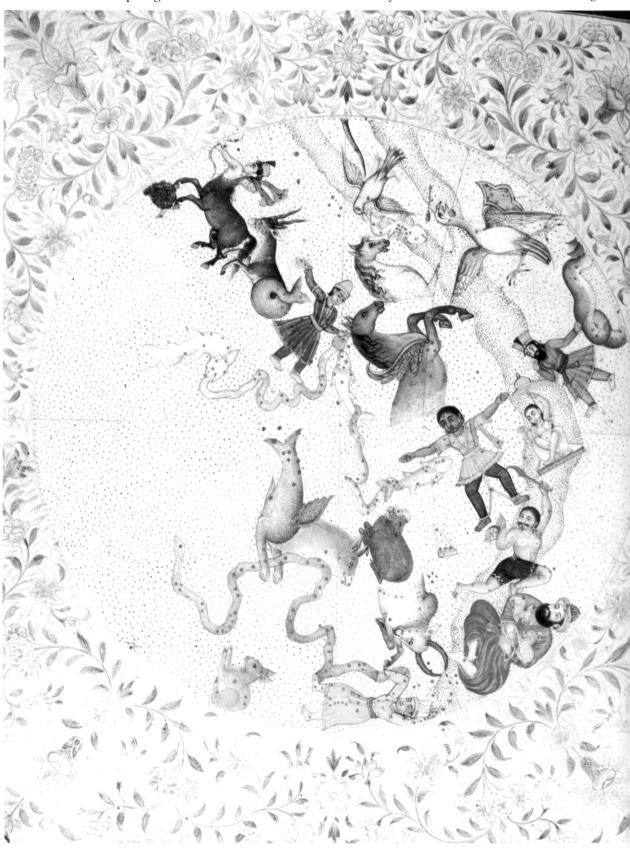

Zodiacal figures from the Jamnapattra of Prince Navanibal Singh. Astrological concepts spread from Rome and Byzantium to India. Sanskrit MS OR 5259. British Museum, London.

there via the Pacific islands, but we must wait upon historians and archaeologists for a definite answer.

Except where Africa has encountered the arts of Hindu astrologers through the settlement of Indians and Pakistanis on its east coast, astrology seems to be little known there. In South Africa, however, the Dutch Reformed Church frowns on stargazing as being contrary to the teachings of God, and has even banned one prediction column in an Afrikaans newspaper. Besides some itinerant charlatans and money-seekers, there are a number of reputable students of the British Faculty of Astrological Studies, who practise their art quietly, and whose clients mainly seem to be English-speaking and female.

Non-European South Africans appear to be interested in the star forecasts of newspapers, most of which are syndicated, and must have even less application than usual for such readers.

One of the best-known Australian astrologers is L. Furze-Morrish, whose works are widely read in England and the United States. The Australian Theosophical Society gives classes in astrology. However, although there are a number of serious astrologers – as well as those ubiquitous star columns in the papers – in general the Australians seem uninterested in the subject. American astrology is too diffuse to be dealt with here, and we shall be examining some of its aspects in the chapters relating to nineteenth- and twentieth-century customs.

The Dark Ages

The Emperor Julian the Apostate encouraged Mithraism and was greatly interested in astrology. Statue. Museo Capitolino, Rome.

Temple of Mithras under the Church of St Clement in Rome. Mithraism held that each planetary sphere governed aspects of personality.

History is an unending drama, but its eras—unlike the acts within a play—do not end neatly separated from the next by a curtain. Thus, while the Roman Empire was collapsing into final chaos, yet still retaining its powerful thrall over the minds and bodies of peoples in many lands, a tiny beacon was beginning to light the darkness. This was the new Christianity.

Its followers came from every sort of background, and were naturally strongly influenced by the beliefs of their forebears which they tried to reconcile with the new faith. Since the Church Fathers could never hope to eradicate all ideas so deeply embedded in the minds of the new Christians, they borrowed and transformed some pagan customs, while denigrating many practices like astrology as heresy or works of the devil. This frequently prevented further exploration and discussion of existing knowledge, and temporarily brought to a halt scientific and philosophical development in western Europe. Thus classical wisdom was entrusted to the care of Jewish and Muslim scholars, who were eventually responsible for returning it to Europe by way of southern Spain.

Pagan deities became the foundation for Christian demons, although some—suitably transfigured—were to share many of the attributes of later saints. Where possible pagan shrines acquired respectable Christian associations, and high Christian festivals were celebrated on dates long dedicated to pagan and astrological rites. Curiously enough this resulted in the preservation rather than the eradication of the oldest traditions, so that an age like ours—far divorced from the first principles of any beliefs—is still dimly linked to those ancient ideas.

Before we examine how the early Christians reacted to astrology we must look at the attitudes of Mithraism and Judaism. The former became popular from the first century A.D. and almost supplanted Christianity in its initial stages, and the latter was the precursor and contemporary of the Christian faith.

Mithraism

This religion, which centred on the sun-god, Mithras, the deity of light and truth, had spread westwards from Chaldean and Persian sources, bringing with it astrological customs. Signs of the zodiac are to be found among the carvings in the ruined temples of Mithras. The secret rites were known only to the cult's devotees, many of whom were Roman soldiers, thus explaining how the faith spread to the very outposts of the Roman Empire. As Roman power ebbed the religion declined. This factor and its exclusion of women may account for its demise, and it is also true that the worshippers of Mithras

did not go in for the fervent proselytizing associated with the early Christians. Many Mithraic customs are very similar to those of Christianity, including the celebration of its founder's birthday on the 25th December—the time of the winter solstice—and keeping Sunday as its holy day.

The religion attained its zenith about A.D. 275 and was toppled by Christianity in the fourth century. During his reign (331–363) the emperor Julian, known as the Apostate, tried to replace Christianity with Mithraism, and he was enthusiastic about astrology, which he claimed to have learnt without books or teachers.

Mithraism holds that the soul descends from heaven to earth, travelling through the planetary spheres and gaining characteristics particular to each of them. After death the soul makes a return journey, shedding those appetites acquired on earth: to the Moon go personality defects; to Mercury avarice; to Venus sexual desire; to the Sun intelligence; to Mars bellicose enthusiasm; to Jupiter ambition; and to Saturn laziness. In the eighth sphere it dwells in the heaven of the gods. This journey was symbolized by a ladder composed of different metals corresponding to each planet.

The Jewish Tradition

When we considered how many of the great works, containing the religious and philosophical tenets of particular civilizations, make countless references to astrology as part-science and part-theology, it is strange to note how few are to be found in the Old Testament. Certainly, there are warnings to the Jewish people against dabbling in occult matters. In chapter 18 of Deuteronomy we find: 'There shall not be found among you any one that maketh his son or his daughter to pass through the fire, one that useth divination, one that practiseth augury, or an enchanter, or a sorcerer, or a charmer, or a consulter with a familiar spirit, or a wizard, or a necromancer. For whosoever doeth these things is an abomination unto the Lord.'

The sign of Capricorn, from a synagogue at Dura-Europus. First or second century A.D. Musée du Louvre, Paris.

While the surrounding societies looked to the heavens and reacted to their signs in Jeremiah the Jews are advised: 'Thus saith the Lord, Learn not the way of the nations, and be not dismayed at the signs of heaven; for the nations are dismayed at them.' After the Jews had erred from their laws the good king Josiah set out to destroy all signs of pagan practices: 'And he put down the idolatrous priests, whom the kings of Judah had ordained to burn incense in the high places in the cities of Judah, and in the places round about Jerusalem; them also that burned incense to Baal, to the sun, and to the moon, and to the planets, and to all the host of heaven.'

The Magi, known for their role in the story of the birth of Christ, were ancient Persian priests, skilled in astrology and occultism. Painting. Fourteenth-century Roman school, Badia.

LE MAT.

I

LE BATELEUR

II

JUNON.

III

L'IMPERATRICE

IIII

L'EMPEREUR

X

LAROUE DE FORTUNE

The words of the Jewish prophets had little to do with the prognostications of the stargazing priests of other societies, but were rather utterances made during a trance-like state of ecstasy.

From the time of Nebuchadnezzar onwards many Jews lived in Babylon, and we can assume that some studied at the school of astrology, while others must have been interested in, or affected by, current astrological ideas. According to Chaldean tradition the constellation Pisces symbolized the Mediterranean countries. For the Jews Pisces was the sign of Israel and the longed-for Messiah. In his fascinating book *The Bible as History* Werner Keller puts forward the proposition, shared by some astronomers, that the famous Star of Bethlehem was in fact the conjunction of Jupiter and Saturn in Pisces. This occurred three times in one year, and from astronomical calculations it appears that the date of the actual birth of Christianity could be 7 B.C. All civilizations regarded Jupiter as a lucky and regal star, and Jewish custom, based on Babylonian ideas, held Saturn to be Israel's protector. The Roman historian Tacitus also describes Saturn as such. Thus, astrologically minded Jews of that time could not help but be astounded at the signs in the sky. Perhaps, at last, a mighty king was coming to lead them.

The Magi were originally a Persian priestly tribe, skilled in dream-interpretation, astronomy, and astrology. They may have seen the conjunction earlier in the year and, from astronomical and astrological lore, deduced that it would

occur again, and that it was some kind of momentous announcement. Before three of them had come upon the stable at Bethlehem, they had sought out King Herod and asked: 'Where is he that is born King of the Jews? For we have seen his star in the east, and are come to worship him.' Such interest may also have been based upon a horoscope which suggested that a birth of the utmost importance was to take place in that year. It is curious to realize that the early Christian Fathers, while denouncing astrology, had to face the fact that their own faith had come into existence heralded by what can be seen as a significant astrological event.

After the dispersion in A.D. 135 the Jews could be found spread over a wide area. Many eventually settled in southern Spain, where Jewish and Arabic doctors were particularly prized by Moorish, and later Christian, rulers. Between the twelfth and fourteenth centuries, medicine, mathematics, and astrology were all inter-related, and thus Jewish scholars had a profound influence over astrological matters. Woven into medical practice were the ancient ideas that parts of the body were affected by specific planets, that medicinal herbs should be picked at certain times in the moon's cycle or under particular signs, and that illness must be treated after examining the birth chart. Many Jews knew Arabic and Greek, and were responsible for translating classic Greek works on astrology, copies of which they had brought with them from the libraries of Byzantium and Alexandria.

The Reader of the Synagogue of Toledo, Isaac

XI

LA FORCE

XII

LE PENDU

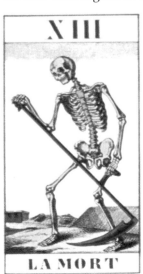

XIII

LA MORT

XIIII

TEMPERANCE

XV

LE DIABLE.

XVI

LA MAISON DE DIEU

V — JUPITER.

VI — L'AMOUREUX.

VII — LE CHARIOT

VIII — LA JUSTICE

VIIII — L'ERMITE

Ibn Sid, edited the famous astronomical tables, known as the *Alfonsine Tables*, after King Alfonso X, the Wise, of Leon and Castile. These regularized astronomical calculations through the Middle Ages and, until the building of the Greenwich Observatory, longitude and latitude were roughly estimated from Toledo. Another Jewish scholar, Abraham Ben David, believed that God had given man's fate to the stars, but that the individual's own intellect could help counteract their adverse powers. Nahmanides, a thirteenth-century doctor at the court of Barcelona, defended astrology as a science, holding that the stars controlled man's destiny, while prayer and virtuous living could minimize whatever misfortunes fate had in store.

Not all great Jewish scholars were in favour of astrology. Moses Maimonides, who was born in Cordoba and later became Saladin's personal physician, was wholly sceptical and wrote: 'Anyone who has faith in these and similar things and believes in his heart that they contain truth and wisdom but that the Torah has forbidden them, belongs to the fools and the senseless and is to be classed with women and children.'

Perhaps the most famous of Jewish writings to influence astrological traditions was the Cabbala. This is a collection of doctrines supposedly handed down by Moses to the rabbis. Basically, it is a mystical commentary on the Torah (the first five books of the Old Testament) and is among the oldest systems of mystical thought, once regarded as the key to all the mysteries of the universe. As such it has strongly attracted and influenced philosophers,

religious thinkers, astrologers, alchemists, and magicians from every kind of faith, through the Dark Ages down to the present day. Its origins are obscure, but it may owe something to the Egyptian mystery cults. The Cabbala is chiefly composed of two works: the *Book of Formation*, written between the second and sixth century A.D., and the *Book of Splendour*, mainly produced in Spain by Moses Leon around 1275.

The creators of the Cabbala must have been familiar with the philosophies of Aristotle and Pythagoras, for they shared the concept of planetary correspondence. Twelve of the thirty-two Paths of Concealed Glory, which are the foundations of Cabbalistic thought and meditation, are given zodiacal and planetary correspondences. The zodiac represents stages of experience through which the human soul must constantly pass. Similar correspondences are to be found in the twenty-two trumps of the intriguing tarot pack, also influenced by the Cabbala.

Moses Leon's words are certainly an echo of astrological attitudes we have already encountered: 'There are seven planets corresponding to the seven firmaments, and by them all the world is regulated. The words "let there be light" refers to the moon, and "let them be for lights" indicates the sun. They should be for seasons, because seasons, holy days, new moons, and sabbaths are determined by them. The supernatural worlds are above them. There are two worlds, an upper world and a lower world, the lower being on the pattern of the upper.'

The twenty-two trump cards of the tarot. No one really knows when the tarot cards came into existence. They are still used in fortune-telling and in a game called 'tarocchini', popular in Italy and central Europe. The twenty-two cards are linked to the paths in the Cabbala and are therefore associated with the mystical aspects of astrology.

XVII. — L'ÉTOILE

XVIII — LA LUNE

XVIIII — LE SOLEIL

XX — LE JUGEMENT

XXI — LE MONDE

This, and many other astrological works, had an enormous appeal for scholars of other faiths, and many upright Christians must have felt that their own learned men, who dabbled in the wisdom collected and sustained by Jewish and Arab scholars, were in grave danger of damnation. Thus, in the twelfth and thirteenth centuries the teachers at the young universities in western Europe had to face the task of reconciling the learning of the ancients, which incorporated much astrological lore, with the doctrines of the Church Fathers, who had frowned on such paganism.

The Attitude of the Church

The opening centuries of the Christian era were riddled with what later became viewed by the orthodox as heresies. From our standpoint it is easy to see that the thinkers of such sects were merely trying to fuse the new Christianity with existing doctrines, mainly those taken from oriental and Greek philosophies, particularly the metaphysical ideas of Pythagoras and Plato.

Despite the clear dating which begins 'anno domini' Christianity and other faiths were destined to overlap for a long while.

Until the anti-astrological pronouncements of St Augustine, one of the greatest influences on Church attitudes, Christian writers did what they could to reconcile their beliefs with those which included astrological principles. We can obtain some idea of how some early Christians accepted astrology from the apocryphal Christian work *The Clementine Recognitions*, which purported to be the writing of one Clementine to James, the brother of Jesus, dealing with the activities of a small group of Christians between the time of the Crucifixion and the Resurrection. Probably dating back to the second century A.D., it described astrology as the science of 'mathesis' —a mental exercise to gain knowledge. In this work the patriarch Abraham was said to be an astrologer, who, through his comprehension of the system of stars, recognized the Creator, while the rest of mankind were in ignorance.

One of these heretical sects was the Gnostics,

The synagogue at Toledo. The Jewish and Arab scholars who lived in Spain in the early centuries of Christianity did much to preserve and foster the learning of the ancient world, including knowledge of astrology.

TERRÆ·MO·TVS

whose chief centre was at Alexandria. Incidentally, Alexandria, and those regions to come under Islamic rule, kept astrology alive while it declined in the west between the fifth and twelfth centuries. According to Gnostic belief, when a new person was born the soul descended from heaven and had to pass through the whirling crystalline spheres of Pythagoras' philosophy, which the Gnostics no longer viewed as mathematical concepts but as barriers between man and heaven. In every sphere the soul acquired characteristics that dulled its perfection. After death, the archon (or ruler) of each sphere tried to prevent the soul from returning to its divine source. Gnostics believed that the influence of the stars over men's destiny was evil. We should not be too surprised at their reasons for reaching this conclusion. Since the early Christians were busy transforming Olympian deities into demons, a pagan practice like astrology could easily become charged with malevolent influences.

The great stumbling block for early Christians was the determinism imposed by belief in astrology. Fundamentally, from their point of view astrology would have to be mistaken since, instead of a single omnipotent Creator, it permitted numerous gods as well as the forces of nature to direct man's will. If God was the sole controller of the universe it was impossible that the stars should be the cause of man's destiny. Writing in the fourth century, St Ephrem demonstrates this perplexity: 'If God is just He can not have set up genethliac stars whereby men would necessarily become sinners.'

The Star of Bethlehem was a particular astrological hurdle for those Christians who wanted both to deny the validity of divination by the celestial bodies and claim its demonic origins. For St Jerome, living early in the Christian era, there seemed to have been little difficulty. He allowed the Magi to be proper astrologers. It was later tradition that changed them into Wise Kings. The Church Fathers, who were nothing if not astute in their devotions,

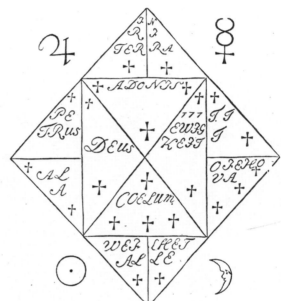

Cabbalism included astrological concepts in its complex lore. This cabbalistic diagram was intended to raise and control all evil spirits invoked to find lost treasure.

Thirteenth-century marble intarsia floor, San Miniato, Florence. The zodiac pattern shows strong Arab influence.

This beautiful and typically Persian plate, 1563–4, was signed by Abd al-Wahid. The traditional zodiac figures were adopted by the Arabs who were deeply influenced by astrology, and the idea of fate. Staatliche Museen, Berlin.

Opposite page:
St Augustine in his study by Botticelli. Uffizi Gallery, Florence.

concluded that the star over the stable was a genuine example of astrology, but nothing to do with the kind of thing dreamt up by charlatan astrologers: it was a sign and not a cause. While the star has a definite place in St Matthew's Gospel, and in the minds of most Christians, it is hard to see how the Church Fathers regarded the New Testament book, the Revelations of St John the Divine, which is richly larded with mystical visionary details, many of which have strong astrological and zodiacal connotations.

From Alexandria sprang the philosophy of Neo-Platonism—one of Christianity's rivals as well as its subtle modifier—which attempted to combine eastern and western concepts in a marriage of Platonic philosophy and oriental mysticism. Among its chief exponents was Plotinus, born in A.D. 205 in Egypt of Greek parents, who later emigrated to Italy, and it was this New-Platonist who propounded a theory

reconciling Christianity and astrology. His theory was that God's will was superior to the influence of the stars, which did not actually cause events on earth, but were merely the signs heralding them. In his own words: 'The active cause is the soul, the inspiration of the great animating spirit.'

Thanks to Plotinus later orthodox Christians like St Thomas Aquinas and certain Renaissance popes could safely become adherents of astrology without falling into theological error, and this may explain why so few astrologers were actually persecuted in later ages when others with apparently inexplicable skills suffered horribly.

We must not imagine that astrology simply slipped into a longer period of hibernation under Christianity. Even while St Augustine was decrying it, astrology still had its learned Christian apologists, whose works must have

Zodiac circle, hour glass, learned book and crystal ball are the equipment of this Arab astrologer. Early seventeenth-century border design from a folio of 'Jehangir's Album'.

Royal astrologer with instrument. Miniature from Arabic manuscript of Allah al-Kaswir's 'Cosmographie', written in Damascus in 1390.

been read at the same time as those of the Church Fathers. The *Mathesis*, a fourth-century work by an intellectual and aristocratic Roman, Julius Firmicus Maternus, is still regarded as a classic of its kind. Maternus believed that the astrologer should lead an upright life because he arbitrated between souls and celestial beings. For him the human soul was a spark of the divine mind which exercises its power through the stars.

Another Christian, and one who eventually became a bishop, was Synesius of Cyrene. He considered the study of astrology to be a preparation for the more elevated study of theology. He reasoned that astrology could be accepted because history repeats itself, since the stars return to their former positions. According to Synesius the universe is a whole, and its parts are bound together by sympathy. Such a theory was echoed and developed in the twentieth century by the psychologist C. G. Jung.

However, while these learned and sincere men did their best to keep astrology alive and respectable they had little power to influence the formidable bishop of Hippo, St Augustine (354–430). His view of astrology was paradoxical, rather like his attitude to chastity which he required to be granted him later rather than sooner: he condemned astrology as evil and yet dismissed it as demonstrably invalid. Perhaps his views harked back to his youth during which he admitted to believing in astrology and consulting astrologers. In *The City of God*, which St Augustine wrote after the fall of Rome in A.D. 410, he stated: 'Those who hold that stars manage our actions or our passions, good or ill, without God's appointment are to be silent and not to be heard . . . For what doth this opinion but flatly exclude all deity. . . .' While agreeing that certain astrological predictions proved correct he explained that although astrologers 'so often found answers which are wonderfully true, it is not because of their imagined art, but through inspiration of demons.'

Astrology for the Church Fathers was immoral

rather than incorrect, but early Christianity was inclined to frown on any kind of science as heresy simply because it was science. In a letter, St Augustine wrote that it was better to ignore the mistakes of astrologers 'than to be forced to condemn and repudiate the divine laws or even the supervision of our own household.' He cites a rather neat and amusing example of how if an astrologer absolutely believes in his calling he must apply the law of the stars to his own hearth. Thus, if he berates, or even beats his wife, not for any real infidelity, but for something trivial like looking too long out of a window, she is entitled to rebuke his harshness with his own philosophy, saying he should beat Venus rather than her since it was this planet that influenced her behaviour.

The fatalism of Greek philosophy, Neo-Platonism, and the Gnostic Christians was quite contrary to St Augustine's vigorous doctrine of free will. However much he railed against astrology he never went as far as trying to ban it: something which might have been virtually impossible since the concept of the zodiac was

The Arab astrologer Albumazar who made a distinction between the influence of the planets and fixed stars.

Gemini. One of a set of the twelve signs of the zodiac from 'The Book of Stars and Constellations', a seventeenth-century Persian manuscript. Spencer Collection, The New York Public Library.

by now deeply embedded in mens' minds.

Probably because of strong Greek and eastern influences that other great Christian centre, Byzantium, seemed to find astrology perfectly acceptable. Constantine, its founder, had died a Christian, but his city had been consecrated according to pagan rites, and an astrologer had drawn its birth chart. Astrology was obviously a popular and flourishing business in Byzantium, and even the famous chariot races were influenced by the apparent dictates of the planets.

While our thoughts are turned eastwards we might look at how the contemporary Arab world reacted to astrology. In fact most of their science seemed to be connected in some part with it. The renowned doctor, Avicenna (980–1037), used astrological computations in his medical practice.

In the city of Baghdad, the caliph Harun al-Rashid built a great observatory for astronomical and astrological purposes. This was used by the famous astrologer Albumazar, whose book on the subject contained the grammar and technicalities of the Greek and Egyptian astrological traditions. Albumazar also tried to settle the problems posed by the Neo-Platonists: namely the amount of influence wielded by the planets, and how much free will man might exercise over his own destiny. However, he left matters in such a complicated state that astrologers could find neatly argued escape-routes, should a client's fate and horoscope diverge. Although the Arabs produced a large selection of written material on astrology, they seemed to lack Greek inventiveness, and after the twelfth century allowed the subject to slip into the realm of magic.

Towards the end of the tenth century the caliphate of Baghdad was declining, but Muslim rule was to flourish in Spain for another two centuries. Spain was Islam's stepping-stone into

The Moon and Jupiter in Sagittarius, with the five other planets below. From an astrological treatise by Albumazar. Thirteenth-century Arabic manuscript. Bibliothèque Nationale, Paris.

Opposite page:
This fourteenth-century illumination depicts how individual planets were related to great men who were ruled by them. Österreichische Nationalbibliothek, Vienna.

The comet that appeared in 1066 may well have been taken as an omen of ill-fortune by the English. Whatever the attitude of the Church, the appearance of any unusual phenomenon in the sky generally caused apprehension among common people. Detail from the Bayeux Tapestry.

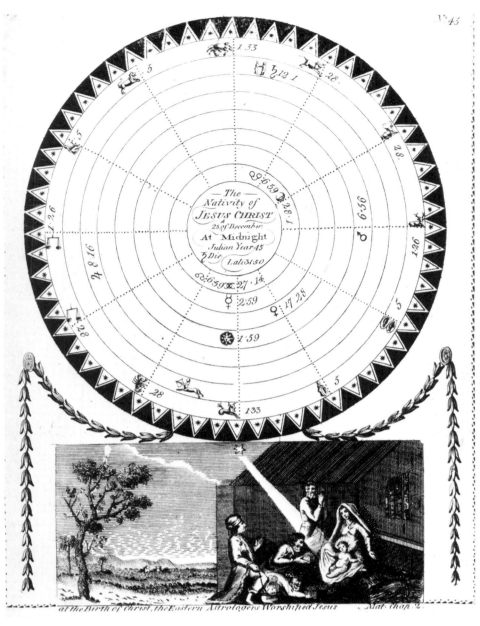

Although later astrologers tried their hand at drawing up the horoscope of Christ the early Church Fathers regarded such an act as heretical. Horoscope of Jesus from 'A Complete Illustration of the Occult Sciences' by Ebenezer Sibly, 1790.

Mercury, the messenger of the gods. The planet Mercury was believed to be the ruler of Christianity, and by the thirteenth century pagan and Christian ideas were inextricably linked. Statue by Gian Bologna. Museo Nazionale, Florence.

Europe, and this was one of the major paths by which the ancient knowledge of astrology and astronomy was passed back to the West. At the end of the tenth century a certain Gerbert, who had been educated in Spain, became Pope Sylvester, and thus took his knowledge and interests to Italy. This pope was particularly interested in astronomy, and even converted one of the towers of the Lateran Palace into an observatory. Many of his contemporaries, however, must have felt sure he had darker motives, for he earned a sinister reputation as a magician. However, it was largely through Sylvester's influence that the Pythagorean concept of a spherical universe, composed of seven spheres, ousted the belief in a flat earth that had possessed the minds of western European thinkers. Although the Pythagorean theory was not correct, it was a step nearer the truth.

In the eleventh and twelfth centuries astrology began to make its comeback in Europe. The Church may still have denounced the practice, but when some momentous prophecy threatened to upset the order of society, even priests and other convinced Christians could not risk ignoring it. In 1179, in the German countries, one John of Toledo published a work predicting that in 1186 all the planets would meet in conjunction in Libra, resulting in frightful tempests and a cataclysm. Wherever the news

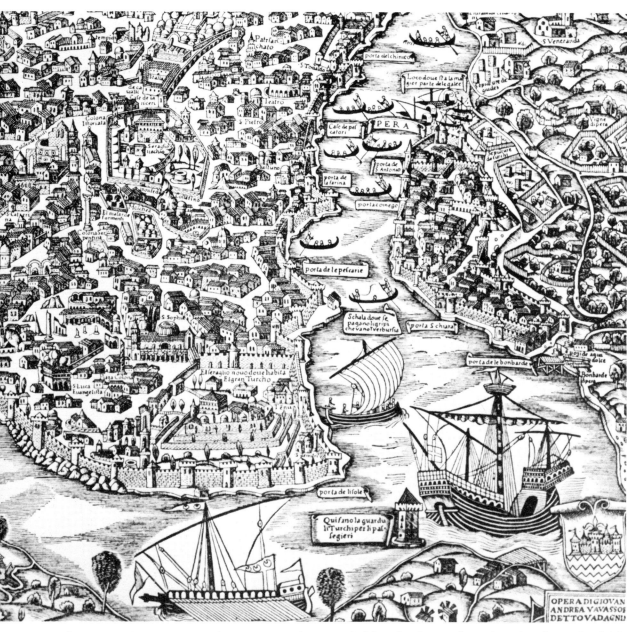

Constantinople, the capital of the Byzantine Empire, where astrology flourished. Sixteenth-century Italian engraving.

spread preparations were made. In Byzantium the windows of the palace were bricked up, in England the Archbishop of Canterbury ordered a fast, and in many other places caves were made ready as hiding-places. Perhaps some terrible storms did rage in that year, but there is no record of them in the then known world.

Once astrology became re-established as a matter of serious study the astrologers divided their subject into eight branches: medicine judicial astrology, agriculture, alchemy, the science of images, the science of mirrors, illusion or magic, and necromancy. The last two hardly enhanced the reputations of astrologers, for they placed their craft firmly in the world of magic, especially in the suspicious minds of clerics. Indeed, some of the more dubious practitioners were probably quack-magicians with a veneer of astrological lore. Naturally, churchmen's attitudes varied and became more flexible, for astrology was becoming so wide-spread as to infiltrate all sectors of leaning: neither mathematics nor medicine could be taught without it. Even the various religions were ascribed to the control of different planets. As we have already learned Judaism belonged to Saturn; Islam was given to Mars and Venus because of its martial and sensual aspects, and its holy day, Friday, was dedicated to Venus. Under Rome, Christianity was believed to be ruled by the Sun and Jupiter, but later the faith was given to Mercury, and the thirteenth-century philosopher, Roger Bacon, thought that Mercury's obscure orbit corresponded to the Christian mysteries. The concept of classical astrological types was also beginning to be generally accepted, and affected all sorts of philosophy and literature. Soon ordinary people understood that a Venus type was a voluptuary, and a Saturnine type was cold and distant,

The brazen head of Friar Roger Bacon whom some accused of being a magician. He was sufficiently interested in astrology to try and find the propitious moment for attending to particular matters.

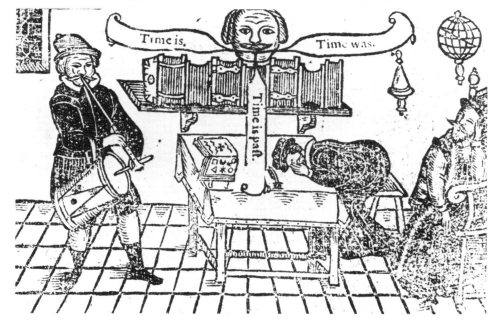

Time is. Time was. Time is past.

whereas the Jupiter type was composed and moderate.

Unwillingly, the Church began to accept the use of astrology in the diagnosis of disease, and the prediction of natural events like the weather, and soon theology admitted that the planets influenced both plants and animals. While opening this door on knowledge the Church firmly slammed all doors on magic and the occult arts, whose practice it prohibited.

The Renaissance of Astrology

Now we are going to meet a host of European savants, writers, astrologers and adventurers, all concerned with the study of the stars at the popular or erudite level. Most upheld the practice of astrology, while some did their utmost to discredit it. In this crowded hall of fame we shall also rub shoulders with princes, rulers and ordinary folk whose daily lives were swayed by the astrological ideas of their age.

In the England of the thirteenth century the new university of Oxford witnessed the rebirth of learning. Its first recorded chancellor, Robert Grosseteste, held astrology in great esteem and thought it could be used in almost anything from agriculture and alchemy to medicine and weather forecasting.

Grosseteste's famous pupil was the Franciscan monk, Roger Bacon (1219–1294), who, after his death, earned somewhat unjustly the reputation as a dabbler in the occult. It was certainly true that he sought to justify magical practices and to trace the association between ancient magic and astrology, which he wrote about in his *Speculum Astronomiae*. This work caused him to be imprisoned through the influence of the head of the Franciscan order. Bacon, like most learned men of his time, was influenced by the Cabbala, and involved in what we might call experimental science. He particularly valued the use of observation in scientific matters, and experimented in optics and alchemy. Such studies at that time would naturally include astrology, in which Bacon found two main differences: one had to do with magic, and the other was concerned with the proper application of judicial astrology. He believed that the true astrologer should not deal in prophecy but should use his science to determine reasons and possibilities, nor did he share the fatalism of contemporary astrologers.

By the time of Geoffrey Chaucer (1340–1400), we can see that the ordinary English people were well acquainted with popular astrology, for that poet's picture of contemporary life *The Canterbury Tales* is spiced with astrological references, which must have been perfectly intelligible to its readers. In the 'Prologue' the doctor of physic is credited with sound astrological knowledge, and the Wife of Bath explains her amorous life in terms of her stars.

In the 'Franklin's Tale' Chaucer shows his scorn at unscrupulous stargazers, and describes in some detail how an astrologer performs his calculations in order to dupe a young client. In

Geoffrey Chaucer. His most famous work. 'The Canterbury Tales' provides us with a colourful picture of contemporary life and contains many references to popular astrology. Henry E. Huntington Library and Art Gallery, San Marino, California.

Far right:
The Wife of Bath from 'The Canterbury Tales' who blithely blamed her temperament on the influence of Venus. Henry E. Huntington Library and Art Gallery, San Marino, California.

many of the other tales the characters' successes are said to be helped by the position of the planets in particular houses. Descriptions of time also have strong astrological/astronomical overtones:

The yonge sonne hath in the Ram his halfe course y-run.

Although Chaucer claimed to know relatively little about astrology, he was able to compose a treatise on the astrolabe.

The Count of Bollstädt (1206–1280), born in Swabia, and known more widely as the Dominican Albertus Magnus, was a famous scholar and philosopher who upheld the Aristotelian view of philosophy, which meant accepting astrology. He believed that astrologers stood on safe ground only so long as they predicted events subject to natural causes and wrote: 'Any astrologer who did this does not commit a fault but rather serves a useful purpose and saves many things from harm. Anyone who predicts the future arbitrarily is a deceiver and to be shunned.' These are strong words indeed from the scholar who believed in the magical power of herbs. The popular work *The Secrets of Women* was attributed to the hand of Albertus Magnus. This contained such information as that each month during its nine in the womb a child is controlled by a different planet which bestows various attributes, and that deformed children are caused by constellations.

Albertus Magnus is also well known for having as his pupil St Thomas Aquinas (1225–1274), who gave astrology the accolade of respectability, since his Thomist system of logic influenced Western Christianity for many centuries. He, too, was a Dominican, and an adherent of Aristotelian philosophy, which he managed to interpret in accordance with Christian doctrine, so legitimately admitting a pagan philosopher into the confines of Christianity.

St Thomas Aquinas. This Dominican monk had much to do with making astrology acceptable in Christian Europe. Painting by Fra Angelico. Museo di San Marco, Florence.

Left:
Dante condemned personal prediction as impious, but used the symbolism of astrology in his 'Divine Comedy'. Painting by Domenico di Francesco. Florence Cathedral.

This fifteenth-century fresco was designed by the Duke of Ferrara's court astrologer and painted by Francesco del Cossa. March is a young girl, Spring, over Aries. Palazzo Schifanoia, Ferrara.

Saturn, traditionally depicted as an old man with a scythe. The ruling planet of Scotland, it controls Capricorn and Aquarius. Illustration from a work by Guido Bonatti (1491).

We can perhaps imagine how surprised Aristotle and the early Church Fathers would have been to meet in such circumstances.

Aquinas agreed that the stars had influence over men's bodies, for they acted as the Creator's intermediaries, but neatly left a clause for the necessary exercise of free will, whereby men could master their own baser instincts. While finding the use of astrology perfectly justified for predicting the weather and medical purposes, he criticized the making of personal predictions, and wrote: 'Few indeed are the wise who can control their own passions and predilections and prophesy correctly'; and: 'If anyone employs the observation of the stars for predicting fortuitous events, or such as happen by chance, or even predicting with certainty man's future actions, he does so falsely.' Should an astrologer do this Aquinas claimed that he had invoked demonic powers.

Italy

The considerable influence of Thomist doctrine over the Italian poet Dante (1265–1321) may be

Lodovico Sforza, Duke of Milan, and patron of artists, was a firm believer in astrology. Painting by Leonardo da Vinci, Milan.

seen in the *Divine Comedy*. Like the sainted doctor Dante condemned astrologers who practised the art of personal prediction not because they were in error but because they were impious. *Paradise* is rich in current astrological and astronomical lore, and in it Dante acknowledged his own birth sign, Gemini, as the donor of his talent:

O stars of glory, from whose light on high
A mighty virtue poureth forth, to you
I owe such genius as doth in me lie;

In *Purgatory* the poet asks one of the tormented spirits about the causes of vice, and receives this answer:

By you who live, causation's all assigned
To the sole stars, as though they could compel
Into their own fixt paths all things combined.
If that were so, it would destroy free will
Within you, and it were unjust indeed
You should have joy for good or grief for ill.
Promptings of motion from your stars proceed—
I say not all, but if I did, what then?
Light's given you to know right from wrong at
 need.
And free will, so its stuff can stand the strain
Of its first tussles with the stars, will fight,
If nourished well, to win the whole campaign;

For a nobler nature, mightier might,
You're the free subjects—might which doth
 create
A mind in you that's no star's perquisite.
So, if the world now goes with crooked gait
The cause is in yourselves for you to trace;

St Augustine would have approved of such an answer, but to admit that man's free will had to do battle with the stars is to acknowledge that those same stars did exercise great power.

Dante demonstrated just what he thought of professional astrologers (and other sorts of magicians) when he confined Guido Bonatti to the fourth chasm in the eighth circle of hell in the company of the Scottish wizard Michael Scott. Both are depicted with their heads turned permanently backwards as punishment for trying to divine the future.

Guido Bonatti was one of the best-known professional astrologers of the thirteenth century. From the beginning of the renewed interest in astrology Italy led the way. This was perhaps because of the questioning attitude of Italian scholars towards theology, and also because it was in Italy that the passionate interest in antiquity which brought about the flowering of the European Renaissance was born. Professors

Celestial Map from 'Harmonia Macrocosmica' by Andreas Cellarius (1661). A Ptolemaic view of the universe. Baynton-Williams Gallery, London.

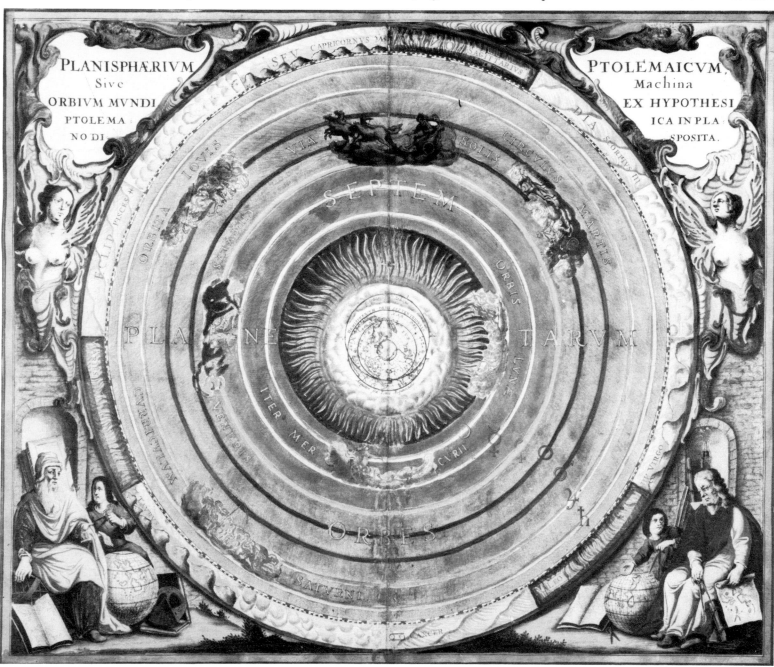

of astrology were found in Italian universities between the thirteenth and sixteenth centuries and Bologna is said to have had a chair of astrology as early as the twelfth century. So it was no wonder that Bonatti had among his clients nobles and warlords, like the Ghibelline leader Guido da Montefeltro, whom he helped to win battles against the Guelfs with his astrological advice. Once in his capacity as adviser Bonatti was bested by a peasant who declared it would rain, while the astrologer swore that it would not. The fact that it did rain did not seem to damage the astrologer's reputation, for the Republic of Florence employed him, and the hard-headed Florentine merchants were not given to paying out gold for illusory gains.

His Latin work *Liber Astronomicus*, which became popular among amateur and professional astrologers, contained a mixture of Greek and Arabic knowledge, enriched with mythology and his own ideas. Even when later scientific discoveries showed much of it to be nonsense the book continued to be read avidly, and was translated into English by the astrologer William Lilly in 1676, ten years after Newton had discovered gravitation! In this book Bonatti offended both doctors and priests, for he set the astronomer/astrologer above them in wisdom, and also revealed that members of the clergy, despite their denigration of the science, were not above consulting astrologers. Bonatti's use of astrology was not just for very important matters: he suggested it could be employed for finding the right time for almost any enterprise.

To heal the rift between the Guelphs and Ghibellines in his birthplace, Forli, Bonatti persuaded the populace to begin rebuilding the city walls (which had been damaged during the factional fighting) under a constellation appointed by himself. One man from each party was chosen to lay the foundation stones, but when Bonatti gave the signal only the Ghibelline put down his stone. The Guelph refused to play his part because the astrologer was known to be of the opposing side, and might be using this opportunity to harm the Guelphs. Bonatti's angry retort was: 'God damn thee and the Guelph party, with your distrustful malice! This constellation will not appear above our city for 500 years to come.' Not long afterwards the Guelphs of Forli were destroyed, but, as is the way with history, two centuries later their arguments were almost forgotten.

For a man with such far-seeing powers Bonatti was singularly unlucky in the matter of his own death: he was murdered by robbers on the way back to Forli after lecturing on astrology at French and Italian universities. Somehow one feels he would have delayed or altered his journey, if he consulted his own stars.

In Jacob Burckhardt's great work *The Civilization of the Renaissance in Italy* we learn that: 'In all the better families the horoscopes of the children were drawn as a matter of course, and it sometimes happened that for half a lifetime men were haunted by the idle expectation of events which never occurred . . .' The case of the astrologer and doctor, Pierleoni of Spoleto, is a

warning to anyone who relies too much on their own horoscope. He foresaw his own death by drowning, and spent most of his life avoiding water, even refusing work in Venice for obvious reasons. As it happens, he killed himself by drowning after being accused of conspiracy!

Burckhardt also tells us 'The stars were questioned whenever a great man had to come to any important decision, and even consulted as to the hour at which any undertaking was to be begun. The journeys of princes, the reception of

Pope Leo X whose childhood horoscope predicted he would become head of the Church. Painting by Raphael, Galleria Palatina, Florence.

The earth surrounded by the seven planets, and the relationship between the seven days of the week and the planets. Woodcut from an astrological tablet, 1480–90.

foreign ambassadors, the laying of the foundation-stones of public buildings, depended on the answer . . .'

Lodovico Sforza, Regent of Milan, and a hard-headed man in most matters, believed himself an expert on astrology, and tried to do anything important only on days appointed by his astrologers. When Lodovico married Beatrice d'Este, the second daughter of the Duke of Ferrara, on 17th January, 1491, it was because the day had been chosen by his astrologer as one suitable for the conception of an heir: in fact the marriage produced two sons.

It was not only secular rulers who looked to the stars for guidance. Whatever the original views of the Roman Catholic Church on astrology, the popes of the fifteenth and sixteenth centuries had their court astrologers whom they honoured and whose advice they took seriously. The politically minded Julius II chose the day for his coronation in accordance with the dictates of his astrologer, and refused to leave Bologna for Rome until an astrologically fortunate day. The court of Leo X particularly respected astrologers. This is not surprising when we know that Leo had been Giovanni de'Medici before his elevation to the papal throne and that when he was a small boy his horoscope had predicted he would become pope. Paul III would not hold a consistory until the right time had been selected by the astrologers, which virtually meant that the inner workings of the Church were relying on a pagan practice.

Not everybody favoured astrology. The sixteenth-century historian in the service of the Medicean popes, Francesco Guiccardini, wrote: 'The astrologers do not know what they say. They are right only by chance.' Well before then the great poet and scholar Petrarch (1304–1374) listed astrologers among the people he disliked most, and seemed to know enough about their arts to describe graphically the kind of deceptions they employed. He even engaged in an acrimonious public argument with the astrologer of the Visconti family although they both lived under the Duke of Milan's patronage.

Florentine chroniclers displayed their own scepticism while recording how most of their compatriots allowed themselves to be governed by astrology, and declared it and other superstitions to be vices inherited from their Roman ancestors. One of them wrote: 'No constellation can subjugate either the free will of man or the counsels of God.' It was over this that scholars, astrologers and clerics argued through medieval and Renaissance times.

Support for astrology occasionally provoked the ire of the Church if it thought that its rulings on such practices had been over-stepped. Some of the writings of the physician Arnold of Villanova, and Peter of Abano (also of Padua), who was a believer in astrological images and medicine, were declared heretical. Among these heretical acts was the retrospective drawing of Christ's birth chart, which in orthodox minds was linked with predicting the fall of Christianity and the reign of Anti-Christ, said to depend upon the conjunction of Jupiter and the Moon.

Lorenzo de' Medici. This merchant prince and virtual ruler of Florence used astrologers as did most of his contemporaries. Sculpture by Verrocchio. Volpi Collection, Florence.

Cecco d'Ascoli, a teacher of astrology at Bologna and astrologer to the Duke of Florence, had the doubtful distinction of being one of the few astrologers to be burnt at the stake (1327). According to the unfortunate Cecco's teachings, Christ had come to earth in accordance with the laws of astrology which made the Crucifixion inevitable. The Church could hardly permit astrologers to argue that the motion of the planets had brought Christianity into being, and could therefore bring it to an end.

Despite these setbacks there is much evidence of how astrology came into its own in the Renaissance. Ornamenting every aspect of life were astrological emblems. Paintings like the beautiful frescoes at Ferrara and Padua were created which glorified the classical concepts of astrology, and the craftsmen who wrought such masterpieces were patronized by the powerful men of their age whose beliefs they mirrored and shared.

Astute leaders like Cosimo de' Medici and his grandson, Lorenzo, employed astrologers and evidently believed in their skills. In 1478, under Lorenzo's aegis, the Florentine government even allowed astrologers to select an auspicious day for choosing the commander of the Florentine troops, although Florence was at war at the time!

In Lorenzo's brilliant circle of Platonist scholars we encounter two very different attitudes towards astrology. Marsilio Ficino defended it, and drew the horoscope of all the Medici children, including the Giovanni mentioned above. Pico della Mirandola utterly refuted the practice in a clever work which probably impressed the educated more than all the thunderings of Church reformers. He differentiated between astronomical observation and astrology, and objected to the inherent fatalism in the latter, while upholding the philosophy of free will. Pico argued that if the planets truly ruled human fate then they were superior to God, and as such ought to be worshipped instead. He also ventured into simple science by comparing the actual weather against the forecasts of the astrologers. 'I have been taking note of weather conditions for a whole winter and checking them against predictions. On the 130 days or more I made my observations there were only 6 or 7 which agreed with the published prediction.' This sounds familiar, reminding us of present-day long-term weather forecasts which fail to match the real picture. Pico also examined the astrologers' arts closer to home, and his findings added weight to his arguments.

The result of his refutation was that some astrologers ceased to publish, and others sought

to justify their skills by coming down firmly on the side of man's free will. This slight alteration of attitudes in certain spheres may be seen in paintings: where pictures had previously depicted the planets governing men's lives, Raphael's decorations in the Capella Chigi show the gods of the different planets being guided by angels who in turn are receiving benediction from the Creator on high.

France

In the fifteenth century in France, Philippe de Mézières composed a picturesque allegory *The Dream of the Old Pilgrim*, which portrays an aged crone named Old Superstition arguing in favour of astrology against a beautiful young lady named Bonne Foy from the University of Paris. Bonne Foy's argument distinguishes between astrology and astronomy, and she gets the better of Old Superstition, who retires claiming she can still find plenty of believers – not just ordinary folk but among priests and royalty.

Old Superstition's claim was quite justified. In a preface to one of the books by the prominent astrologer, Johannes Lichtenberger, the redoubtable Martin Luther (1483–1546) wrote: 'The signs in heaven and in earth are surely not lacking; they are God's and the angels' work, and they warn and threaten the godless lands and countries and have significance.'

Above:
An illustration from 'Prognosticatio in Latino' by the fifteenth-century German astrologer Johann Lichtenberger showing the 'terrible conjunction' of the planet Jupiter (left) with Taurus and Saturn under Scorpio, which would supposedly bring about some great calamity.

Above left:
Martin Luther, religious reformer and author of a preface to a book on astrology. Woodcut by Lucas Cranach (1552). British Museum, London.

Members of Lorenzo de' Medici's Platonist group. Left: Pico della Mirandola, the humanist, who wrote: 'Astrology stands first among those superstitions of which she is both mother and foster-child'. Centre: Marsilio Ficino, founder of the Platonic Academy in Florence who wrote: 'The heavens don't affect our will but they do affect our bodies'. On the right is the poet and humanist Poliziano. Painting by Cosimo Rosselli. Chiesa di Santo Ambrogio, Florence.

The French Protestant John Calvin showed no sign of sharing Luther's attitude. 'There hath been of long time a foolish curiosity to judge by the stars of all things what should chance unto men, and hence to enquire and take counsel as touching those matters which are to be done. But we will by and by God willing declare that it is nothing but devilish superstition. Yea, and it hath been rejected by common consent as pernicious to mankind. And yet at this day it hath got the upper hand in such sort that many which think themselves witty men, yea and have been so judged, are as it were bewitched therewith.'

Despite the voice of pure reason it is no wonder that so many people were affected by the predictions of astrologers. It must have been as hard for the learned to decide which view to heed, especially when contemporary astrology so frequently involved the prediction of some world-shattering event.

No doubt that should a current weather forecast predict heavy rain and flooding the authorities would anxiously examine sea walls, river banks and such like, while countrymen would make their own preparations. So we should not smile at our Renaissance ancestors' attitudes to such predictions. In 1500 an Italian astrologer, Nifo, claimed to see some terrible flood written in the heavens, its cause being the sins of mankind. Twenty years later Virdung, an Austrian astrologer, noted certain meteors, and considered them omens of a flood which would occur in 1524 during a major conjunction of planets. Astrologers and almanacs added their weight to this fearful prophecy, and the idea of the floods claimed the attention of many savants. People panicked, built boats, and

Combien il est en sue. Si te

moved away to live on higher ground. To be fair to the prophets of doom there was unusually heavy rain that year. and floods, but fortunately nothing on the vast scale predicted.

That Bonne Foy and Pico della Mirandola had declared a difference between astronomy and astrology to the detriment of the latter didn't seem to trouble contemporary men of science. Johann Muller, known as Regiomontanus, and attached to the king of Hungary's court in the mid-fifteenth century provides such an example. While he was a mathematician, and a famous astronomical observer for which purpose he invented special instruments, he also found time to devise a new method of dividing the heavens into twelve houses, and these unequal divisions are still used by some modern astrologers. Paracelsus (Theophrastus Bombastus von Hohenheim, 1493–1541), the Swiss physician, whose investigations, though muddled, were the beginnings not only of medical science but an attempt to understand the workings of the psyche, was no astrologer, but felt that astrology could be used in medicine to release the secrets of the human mind. He wrote: 'The stars force us to nothing, they incline us to nothing. It is said that a wise man rules over the stars: this does not mean that he rules over the stars in the sky but over the powers which are active in his own mental constitution and which are symbolized by the visible stars in the sky.' He believed the brain equated with the moon in the microcosm, which explained why madness increased at the full and new moons.

We must not imagine that the complexities of astrology were the concern of only the highly educated, the well-read, and the wealthy. With the invention of the printing press, knowledge,

95

Paracelsus, the sixteenth-century Swiss alchemist and physician, believed that astrology could be of some help in understanding how the mind worked.

and of course pseudo-knowledge, gradually reached all those who could read, and was also instrumental in making more people literate. In fifteenth-century France *The Kalendar and Compost of Shepherds* appeared, for the amusement and enlightenment of ordinary men. It had a wide circulation in many European cities and was translated into several languages. Its anonymous author put traditional astrological lore into the mouths of shepherds. From this rather endearing work we gain a good idea of everyday accepted astrological beliefs. A picture shows how the seven planets rule man's physiognomy, and which parts of the body are governed by the zodiac signs.

The varieties of people are explained in terms of the planet under which they are born, thus: 'All men and women that be born under the Sun be very fair, amiable of face, and their skin shall be white and tender . . . The children that are born under the Sun shall desire honour and science, and shall sing very pleasantly. And they shall be of courage good and diligent, and shall desire lordship above other people . . . And of all the members in man's body, the Sun keeps the heart as most mighty planet above all others.'

'Such men and women as be born under the Moon shall be lowly and serviceable, and very gentle . . . and they shall be well favoured both man and woman, and their faces shall be full and round . . . They hate lecherous talkers and speakers of ribaldry . . . They shall gladly go arrayed in many coloured clothes, and they shall soon sweat in the forehead. Also they will have great desire to be masters and mistresses over streams, rivers, and floods, and shall devise many proper engines to take fish and to deceive them . . . And the lights and the brains

A countryman's view of the zodiac. Different tasks are under the rule of particular signs. Woodcut from 'Le Coeur de Philosophie' (Paris, 1504).

of man are under the governance of Luna.'

'The fair planet Mercury is lord of speech . . . Who so is born under Mercury shall be subtle of wit and shall be very crafty in many sciences . . . He shall ever follow and resort to them that be of good manners, and shall be fortunate on the sea to use the course of good merchandise. He shall be very gracious, and he shall have harm by women, and when he is married men shall not set so much by him as they did before . . . He will be a very good man of the church or a religious man, and shall not love to go to warfare . . . He shall have a high forehead, a long visage, black eyes, and a thin beard . . .'

Those born under Venus 'shall be a very gay lover, pleasant and delicious . . . They shall love the voice of trumpets, clarions, and other minstrelsy, and they shall be pleasant singers . . . and shall greatly delight in dancing . . . and will use playing at the chess, and at the cards, and desire oft to commune of lust and love, and covet oft sweetmeats and drinks as wine and be oft drunken, and oft desire lechery . . . They shall be of faith, and they shall love others as well as themselves. They shall be liberal to their friends . . .'

'This planet Mars is the worst of all others, for he is hot and dry, and stirs man to be very wilful and hasty at once, and to unhappiness . . . He causes all wars and battles . . . Under Mars are born all thieves and robbers that keep highways and hurt true men, and night workers, quarrel pickers, boasters, and scoffers. He shall be a great walker, and maker of swords and knives, and shedder of man's blood, a lecher and speaker of ribaldry, red bearded, round visaged, and good to be a barber and letter of blood, and to draw teeth, and is perilous of his hands. And he will be rich of other men's goods.'

Jupiter is a 'noble planet . . . very pure and clear of nature, and not very hot, but he is all virtues. And there are fixed in Jupiter two noble signs of love; the one is Pisces and the other is Sagittary, signs of no evil nor unhappiness. This planet may do no evil; he is best of all the other seven. He keeps the liver of man and maintains it joyously.'

'When Saturn reigns there is much theft used and little charity, much lying, and much lawing one against another, and great prisonment, and much debate, and great swearing . . . And old folk shall be very sickly, and many diseases shall reign among people, and specially in the chief hours of Saturn. And therefore this planet is likened to age, as hard, hungry, suspicious, and covetous, that seldom is content with anything. For Saturn is enemy to all things that grow and bear life of nature, for the cold and stormy bitterness of his time . . . He that is born under Saturn shall be false, envious, and full of debate, and full of law. And he shall be cunning in curing of leather, and a great eater of bread and flesh. And he shall have a stinking breath, and he shall be heavy, thoughtful and malicious; a robber, a fighter, and full of covetousness, and yet he shall keep counsel well . . . and he shall love to sin wilfully . . .

As almanacs became the popular reading of simple folk they resembled their counterparts in

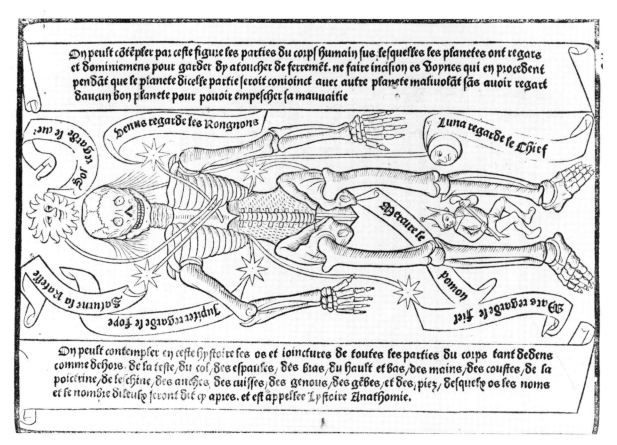

On peult côtêpler par ceste figure les parties du corps humain sus lesquelles les planetes ont regarê et dominiemens pour garder ôp atouscher de ferremêt. ne faire inasion es Bopnes qui en procedent pendât que se planete dicelse partie seroit conioinct auec autre planete maliuosât sâs auoir regart ôaucun bon planete pour pouoir empescher sa mauuaitie

On peult contempler en ceste hyftoire ses os et ioinctures de toutes ses parties du corps tant dedens comme dehors, ôe sa teste, ôu col, ôes espaulles, ôes bras, êu hault et bas, ôes mains, ôes coustes, ôe sa poictrine, ôe seschine, ôes anches, ôes cuisses, ôes genous, ôes gêbes, et ôes piez, ôesquels os les noms et se nombre ôiseuls seront ôit cp apres. et est appelsee L'ystoire Anathomie.

Planetary skeleton. The planets were thought to control the major centres of the body; e.g., Venus ruled the kidneys and Jupiter ruled the liver. Woodcut from 'Icy est le Compost' (1493).

ancient times and other cultures: predictions dealt with the weather; there were farming tips; advice on health – particularly about those illnesses that had astrological connections – and even suggestions for a favourable time to let blood, take a purge, or have a bath!

Of course, the astrologers most remembered are usually those whose patrons were of royal blood, and the court of France, at least until the time of Louis XIV, provided a steady and probably lucrative income for the drawers of birth charts and readers of stars. The royal houses of both Valois and Capet were influenced by astrology. D'Almonsor was an astrologer often consulted by Louis XI (1461–1483), and there is a tale that one night D'Almonsor was visited by two noble gentlemen who demanded that he draw their horoscopes. Death was predicted for both of them: one would die in a chivalrous cause, and the other would probably be poisoned since he seemed threatened by some august person. The former was the Duke of Burgundy, who was killed in battle, and the latter, the Duke of Berry, died soon after, generally thought to have been poisoned by those in the king's service.

The wife of Henry II of France, the cruel and unscrupulous Catherine de Médicis, was interested in all kinds of learning, particularly occult matters, and had great faith in astrology – not surprisingly since her Medici relatives were also strongly influenced by their belief in astrologers. A number of famous stargazers feature in her turbulent life. The first was an Italian, Luc Gaurice – a genuine teacher of mathematics – who cast horoscopes for the Medici clan, and predicted that the child Catherine would become queen of France. When she did in fact become, as wife of the heir apparent, the Dauphine Catherine, she asked Gaurice for advice. He warned the future Henry II to avoid single combat during his forty-first year, for he

was threatened by a head injury which might rob him of sight or life. Henry shrugged off this warning, but his wife did not.

She consulted the most famous prophet of that age, Nostradamus (1503–1566), about Gaurice's prediction. Nostradamus was a learned doctor and astrologer, deeply interested in mysticism and magic. His *Centuries*, first published in 1555, were a collection of enigmatic predictions couched in such obscure terms as to make them more difficult than the most insoluble crossword

Title page to the 'Astrologischer Spiegel' by Johann Georg Sambach (Nuremberg, 1680), showing how the signs of the zodiac affect the body according to the time of birth.

97

Nostradamus showing Queen Catherine of France a vision of the future in a magic mirror. Eighteenth-century print.

Louis XIV visiting the Paris Observatory. His chief minister, Colbert, discouraged the practice of astrology. Engraving by Sebastian Le Clerc. Historical Museum of the Paris Observatory

puzzle, and are open to a wide variety of interpretations. Among these prophecies may be found references to the Great Fire of London, the French Revolution, the rise of the British Empire, the Second Coming of Christ or the end of the world in July 1999, as well as many other events which may or may not have already occurred. None of these would have been as of such overriding interest to Catherine as the quatrains referring to the 'death of the House of Seven', which seemed to prophecy the end of the House of Valois, despite there being seven children, and the following certainly gave support to Gaurice's warning:

The young lion shall overcome the old,
In warlike field in single fight;
In cage of gold he will pierce his eyes,
Two wounds one, then die a cruel death.

Three years after Nostradamus published this Henry II was accidentally slain by a young Scottish captain in a jousting tournament to celebrate the marriage of Henry's daughter. The lance pierced the king's eye, and a splinter from it penetrated his throat: the king's helmet resembled a golden cage.

Ordinary people were not as impressed as Catherine with the prophet's accuracy. They suspected he had caused their king's death, burned his effigy, and demanded the Church should burn the man in person. Fortunately, Nostradamus had a powerful patron in the

Queen Regent, who asked him to draw the horoscopes for her children. He must have been a man of special talent not only to win the queen's favour but to keep it despite the fact that six of those children were destined to have most unfortunate lives. Strictly speaking, the *Centuries* is not a work of astrological computations, but was probably the result of scrying over a bowl of water in much the same way as a medium might use a crystal to concentrate and enter a trance.

Also at the French court during the early sixteenth century was the famous doctor, linguist, and savant Agrippa von Nettesheim (1486–1585), who was particularly interested in occult philosophy. Although he believed the working of the occult sciences to be based on astrology he asked 'why do we trouble ourselves to know whether man's life and fortune depend on the stars? . . . To God who made them in the Heavens and who cannot err, neither do wrong, may we not leave these things.' Later in life, however, he became very much opposed to astrology.

Despite his views Catherine forced him to play the prophet and make astrological predictions, about which he wrote: 'I wish I may predict her something pleasant, but what pleasant prophecies are you to get out of the Furies and Hecate?'

Another astrologer in the service of Catherine de Médicis was the sinister Cosimo Ruggieri, a Florentine, for whom the queen built an observatory. He was also a magician, and a maker of cosmetics and poisons.

Henry IV of France was not as convinced a believer in astrology as Catherine, but when his son was born he had Doctor Roch Le Baillif draw the child's horoscope, and as a reward gave him the title of First Doctor to the King. The night before Henry was stabbed to death by Ravaillac, a religious fantic, an Italian astrologer is alleged to have announced: 'Tomorrow one of the greatest monarchs in Christendom will be slain'.

When Louis XIV was born, Voltaire later recorded, the astrologer Jean Baptiste Morin de Villefranche. who had been waiting outside the queen's bedchamber, rushed off to cast the child's horoscope. This same savant held the chair of mathematics at the Collège de France, and made some of the first serious investigations into longitude.

A Spanish court astrologer predicted that the princess Maria Theresa, would one day be the wife to the greatest king in Europe, and that such a marriage would prevent war. In 1660 she married Louis XIV and their union did in fact avert a war between their two countries. Six years later Colbert, Louis XIV's chief minister, established the Academy of Sciences and prohibited astronomers from studying astrology. Thus the ancient practice slipped out of the hands of the respectable and official sciences into the eager embrace of the populace.

At the age of sixty-six Voltaire published a pamphlet on astrology in which he apologized for still being alive. Two quite separate astrologers had once predicted he would die at thirty-two.

German Calendarium c.1400. The coloured illustrations for each months are accompanied by rules for the hearth, signs of the zodiac, and details of the lengths of days and nights. Sagittarius. MS 15701, British Museum, London.

Voltaire's opinion of astrology is summed up in his description of it as 'This chimaera'. Bust by Houdon. Victoria and Albert Museum, London.

		Augustus	Solis motus Lco		Lune motus medius		Lune Centrum		Lune argumētū medium	
			G m	S G m		S G m		S G m		
c		Petri ad Vincula	18 1	9 16 34	5 3 16	8 12 11				
d	Non	Stephani papę	18 58	9 29 45	5 27 38	9 1 54				
e	Non	Inuentio S. Sephani	19 56	10 12 55	6 22 1	9 18 58				
f	Non		20 54	10 26 6	7 16 24	10 2 2				
g	None		21 51	11 9 17	8 10 47	10 15 6				
A	8 Idus	Sixti papę	22 49	11 22 27	9 5 10	10 28 10				
b	7 Idus	Airę martyris	23 47	0 5 38	9 29 33	11 11 14				
c	6 Idus	Cyriaci & fociorū eius	24 44	0 18 48	10 23 56	11 24 18				
d	5 Idus	Vigilia	25 42	1 1 59	11 18 19	0 7 22				
e	4 Idus	Laurentii martyris.	26 40	1 15 10	0 12 42	0 20 26				
f	3 Idus	Tyburt. martyris.	27 38	1 28 20	1 7 4	1 3 30				
g	2 Idus	Clarę virginis.	28 36	2 11 31	2 1 27	1 16 33				
A	Idus	Hipoliti martyris.	29 34	2 24 41	2 25 50	1 29 37				
b	19 Kal	Septēbris Vigi. Virgo	0 32	3 7 52	3 20 13	2 12 41				
c	18 Kal	Affumptio Marię	1 30	3 21 2	4 14 36	2 25 45				
d	17 Kal		2 28	4 4 13	5 8 59	3 8 49				
e	16 Kal	Octaua Laurentii	3 26	4 17 24	6 3 22	3 21 53				
f	15 Kal	Agapiti martyris	4 24	5 0 34	6 27 45	4 4 57				
g	14 Kal		5 22	5 13 45	7 22 8	4 18 1				
A	13 Kal	Bernardi Conteffous	6 21	5 26 55	8 16 30	5 1 5				
b	12 Kal		7 19	6 10 6	9 10 53	5 14 9				
c	11 Kal	Timothei & Simphoniani	8 17	6 23 17	10 5 16	5 27 12				
d	10 Kal	Vigilia	9 16	7 6 27	10 29 39	6 10 16				
e	9 Kal	Bartholomęi apoftoli	10 14	7 19 38	11 24 2	6 23 20				
f	8 Kal		11 12	8 2 48	0 18 25	7 6 24				
g	7 Kal		12 11	8 15 49	1 12 48	7 19 28				
A	6 Kal	Ruffi martyris.	13 9	8 29 9	2 7 11	8 2 32				
b	5 Kal	Pelagij mar. Auguftini epi.	14 8	9 12 20	3 1 34	8 15 36				
c	4 Kal	Decollatio S. Ioānis Bapti.	15 6	9 25 31	3 25 56	8 28 40				
d	3 Kal	Fœlicis & Adaucti mar.	16 5	10 8 41	4 20 19	9 11 44				
e	2 Kal		17 3	10 21 52	5 14 42	9 24 48				

Auguftus vegetos cados coarcto
Quam poffum bene circulis papyro.

C i

England

Across the Channel in England, during the sixteenth and seventeenth centuries astrology enjoyed a great vogue, and the amount of writings produced by English astrologers demonstrated just how popular was their craft.

From reading the plays and poetry of the period we know just how conditioned readers, playgoers, and writers were to accept, understand, and use astrological concepts. Everyone seemed to be aware that different parts of the body were ruled by the signs of the zodiac, and that there were four humours (body liquids) giving the sanguine, phlegmatic, choleric, and melancholic types, and that these were also under the aegis of the planets and the signs.

Shakespeare's works are full of astrological references – serious, doubting, and jesting. Often characters use the stars to explain away their misfortunes, and all must have been quite familiar to the ordinary playgoer of that time.

In *King Lear* Edmund remarks: 'This is the excellent foppery of the world, that when we are sick in fortune – often the surfeit of our own behaviour – we make guilty of our disasters the Sun, the Moon and Stars: as if we were villains by necessity, fools by heavenly compulsion;

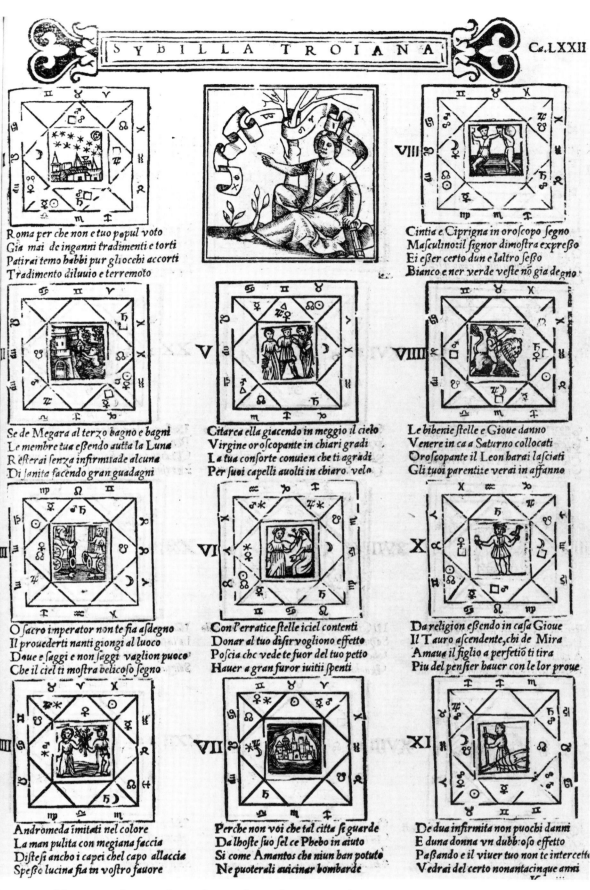

Popular manuals with rhyming quatrains about astrological matters often appeared under the title of some classical-sounding author to lend an air of authority. From 'Triompho di Fortuna', a sixteenth-century Italian work.

knaves thieves and treachers by spherical predominance; drunkards, liars and adulterers by an enforced obedience of planetary influence.' But also in the same play, the difference between Cordelia's character and those of her two sisters is explained thus:

It is the stars,
The stars above us govern our condition . . .

Perhaps one of the best-known Shakespearian astrological quotations is to be found in *Julius Caesar*, when Cassius says:

Men at some time are masters of their fates,
The fault, dear Brutus, is not in our stars,
But in ourselves, that we are underlings.

Astrology appeared in all sorts of everyday matters. The herbalist Nicholas Culpeper considered that herbs were influenced by particular planets which gave them their powers: 'Lily of the Valley . . . under the dominion of Mercury, and therefore it strengthens the brain, recruiting a weak memory, and makes it strong again. Artichokes . . . are under the dominion of Venus, and therefore it is not wonderful if they excite lust. Cucumbers . . . are under the dominion of the Moon, though they are so much cried out against for their coldness, and if they were but one degree colder they would be poison.'

During the sixteenth century there were two

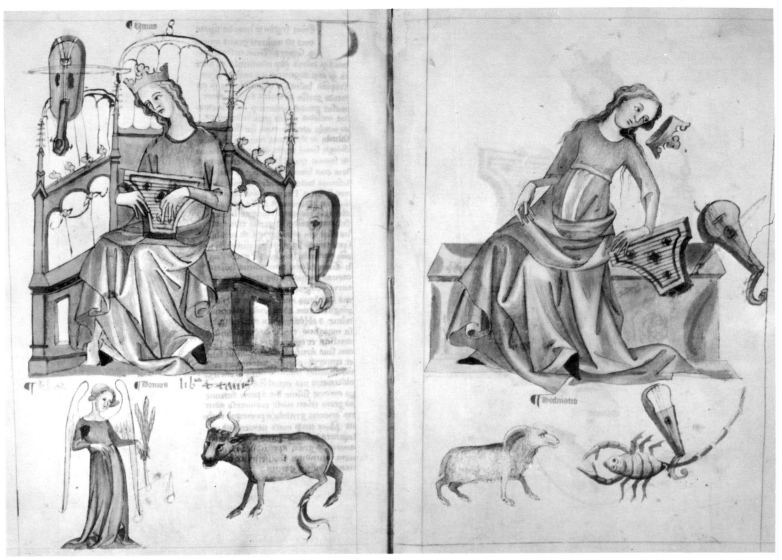

Venus in a good aspect (left) and in a bad aspect. Illustration from a fourteenth-century translation of an Arabic work. Sloane MS 3983, British Museum, London.

NICHOLAS CULPEPER, M.D.
Born Oct 18 1616 Died Jan 10 1654.

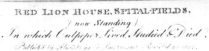

RED LION HOUSE, SPITAL-FIELDS.
(now Standing)
In which Culpeper Lived, Studied & Died.

Nicholas Culpeper, who wrote an 'Astrological Judgement of Diseases'.

famous English royal astrologers who advised the Tudors. The mathematician and astrologer Nicholas Kratzer served Henry VIII. He must have been a scholar to be a friend of Sir Thomas More, and also a wise and diplomatic man to have comfortably survived advising a king whose love life was a stormy one.

Probably the most renowned astrologer was Dr John Dee (1527–1608) who served Henry's three children. He was imprisoned during Mary Tudor's reign for prophesying against her marriage:

Woe to the two nations: Woe and sorrow
Disaster by water: persecution by fire
And the queen shall childless die.

He also forecast that her sister would be queen. Luckily for Dee, he was released, and as soon as she succeeded to the throne Elizabeth recalled his prediction, and commanded him to elect a fortunate day for her coronation.

Besides being an astrologer, crystal-gazer, alchemist, magician, and spiritualist, Dee was a serious mathematician and his calculations helped to inaugurate the Gregorian Calendar in 1583. Yet this man, who was befriended although not really enriched by Elizabeth, was a strange paradox. When he was about fifty he became involved with the charlatan and petty criminal, Edward Kelly. Together they sought the philosopher's stone, attempted to transmute base metals into gold, and indulged in necromancy during which it is said they summoned two angels, Uriel and Michael. Uriel is alleged to have shown Dee the beheading of Mary Queen of

John Dee and Edward Kelly exhibiting their magical skills to Guy Fawkes. Illustration by George Cruikshank.

Scots four years before it actually happened. The two men also travelled abroad where they were no more than fairground hucksters.

However, there must have been much more to Dee's character than naivety or chicanery, for the shrewd Elizabeth trusted him with all kinds of secret negotiations, even asking his advice during the Armada crisis. She tried to get him a living in the Church, but this was opposed by the bishops on the grounds that Dee was a sorcerer. When James I succeeded to the throne Dee lost what positions he had acquired, since the king believed him to be in league with the devil. Nothing was proved for or against the astrologer, who lived out his days at the Mortlake home where once he had entertained the queen, and had been visited by some who wanted to know the future, or others intent on burning him and his magic books.

Astrology left the courts and its practitioners travelled among the ordinary people. Vying for custom and fame, they indulged in abusing one another. One of the best-known popular astrologers was William Lilly (1602–1681) who, being left with a comfortable income, turned to astrology at the age of thirty. He did, however, study for about fourteen years before putting his predictions into print, which is more than can be said for certain of his colleagues, and in 1644 he published two books of prophecies *Merlinus Anglicus Junior* and the oddly titled *A Prophecy of the White King and Dreadful Deadman Explained*. From then on Lilly became a regular producer of almanacs. By licensing

One of William Hogarth's set of twelve engravings, illustrating Samuel Butler's satirical poem 'Hudibras' which caricatures William Lilly.

them the Stationers' Company not only shared in the profits but lent the works a veneer of respectability.

In fact, it was this company that contributed to keeping astrology alive in the mind of the public long after its serious study had fallen into disrepute, for the Stationers' Company maintained a flourishing almanac business well into the nineteenth century. The vague personal predictions to be found between the flimsy covers

of these pamphlets were usually the work of unknown hack writers, trading on astrologers—dubious or respectable—long since dead. The present-day *Old Moore's Almanac* is a descendant of the *Vox Stellarum* of one Francis Moore, who died in 1715. These publications had wide appeal, rather like star columns in today's newspapers and magazines, although genuine astrologers shunned their counterfeit prophecies.

Despite their pagan origins the familiar zodiac symbols were used to embellish churches such as this one at Amiens, France.

greeschafft d̄ hitz/ dz sy alwegē stercke. Zū dē andern mal wirt d̄ Sanguineus glycher dē glentz/ wañ die zyt ist kalt vñ feücht/ darūb ist die cōplexion aller lieplichst/ wañ dz lebē ist im hertzē vnd im feüchte. Sanguineus ist mer geneygt zū boßheit dañ Melācolicus/ vnd flegmaticus ist mer geneygt zū lere/ dañ seine geist seind subtyl/ sy mügen ein ding bald begryffen/ sy ligē den dingen nit ernstlich ob als die flegmatici vñ Melācolici/ sy seind milt buler vnd bulerin/ frölich vñ lachen gern/ sy seind rot vnd dē antlütz vnd singen/ vnd seind etwan kün/ vnd haben vil fleisch/ vnd seind etwan frech vnd tugenthafft/ vnd seind zūgeneygt dem Planeten Jupiter mit seiner natur.

Colericus.

Vnser Complexion ist gantz von feür
Schlaßen vnd kriegen ist vnser abentheür

¶ Der Colericus ist milt/ wañ die feüchtigkeit antzündt im dz blůt vñ dz hertz vnd macht im gilbe vnd dē antlütz. Darum seind die Colerici gar gedürstig/ vñ glychet sich dē sum̄er heiß vnd truckē vnd würt geglychet der vntugendt. Die Complexion ist dryfaltig. Die erst ist hitzig mit einem bleichen antlütz/ dürstig/ sy erschrecken die leüt gern wann sie

truncke sein. Die ander ist sy habē rote antlütz gemischet mit gilbe/ kindig/ vast zornig/ vnnd ran/ durch zyt rot an dem antlütz vnd an den backen/ vnd braun an dem leyb/ vñ auch mit alle Colera glychet sich mit irer natur Mercurio vnd Saturno/ vnd auch iren zeichen/ das ist der wider/ der Leo vnd der Schütz.

Merck das du nitt lassest wann

sich das New antzündt von der Sonnen/ oder wañ der Mon vol ist/ fünff tag vor oder nach/ es sey dañ vast not/ dann im Summer.

Nyemandt sol lassen in den nachgenben tagen/ dañ dauon kompt grosser schaden.
¶ Am ersten tag des Genners/ wer dann laßt der würt krempffig oder stirbt/ oder verleürt das gesicht in dem iar oder verleürt die sinn/ oder wirt reydig.
¶ Wer laßt am achtē kalend des Hornungs/ d̄ stirbt/ oder wirt krempffig/ oder in schlecht das berly.
¶ Wer laßt am achten kalend des Mertzen stirt oder

William Lilly's claim to fame is that he really did, and in ponderous astrological detail, predict the Great Fire of London in his *Astrological Predictions* for 1648.

'In the year 1665 the Aphelium of Mars, who is the general signification of England, will be in Virgo, which is assuredly the ascendant of the English monarchy, but Aries of the Kingdom. When the absis therefore of Mars shall appear in Virgo who shall expect less than a strange catastrophe of human affairs in the commonwealth, monarchy and kingdom of England. There will then, either in or about those times, or near that year, or within ten years, more or less of that time, appear in this kingdom so strange a revolution of fate, so grand a catastrophe and great mutation unto his monarchy and government as never yet appeared of which as the times now stand, I have no liberty or encouragement to deliver my opinion— only it will be ominous to London, unto her merchants at sea, to her traffique on land, to her poor, to all sorts of people, inhabiting in her or to her liberties, by reason of sundry fires and a consuming plague.'

However, such a forecast of doom was just one among many, but Lilly appeared to have a talent to provoke the enmity, or perhaps envy, of a fellow astrologer, Thomas Gataker, who in 1653 produced a pamphlet called *Against the Scurrilous Aspersions of that Grand Imposter Mr William Lillie*, in which he wrote: 'There needs not much skill in his pretended art to discover the vanity of it'; and even more sourly: 'Mr Lillie in all these dreadful Eclipses and malignant Aspects, finds much matter of bad, dismal and disastrous concernment, to Princes, Potentates, Priests, Lawyers, Husbandmen, Graziers, etc. but none at all ever to Wizards, Stargazers, Astrologers, etc. No malignity of any Aspect belike is able to reach them.' One would have imagined someone in Mr Gataker's profession would have been reassured by this, but such was not the case.

A vivid imagination or falsehood? Who can tell? But certainly the Great Fire of London did occur. Lilly was not yet free of suspicion: a

A sixteenth-century popular German work dealing with astrology and the humours. These pages relate to the effects of a choleric temperament and remedies to treat it.

John Drapentier delin et Sculp.

Francis Moore, astrologer and creator of 'Old Moore's Almanac'.

Celestial map showing the movements of the planets with zodiacal and planetary figures, from Andreas Cellarius' 'Atlas Coelestis seu Harmonia Macrocosmica' (1661).

ARATEVM
Compages
DANORVM EX
ARATEA IN
EXPRESSA.

PATRIDGE BICKASTAF

John Partridge, the astrologer, and 'Bickerstaff' who predicted his demise. Contemporary woodcut.

John Gadbury, whose astrological fame rested more on drawing retrospective charts of the famous who were already dead rather than predicting the future.

Parliamentary Committee investigated him to make sure he had not instigated the fire.

This conflagration may have demolished much of London, but it made Lilly's reputation, even though he never again made so successful a prophecy. Fame went to his head, and the advice he published for would-be astrologers is pompous and smug, and smacks more of some book of etiquette than the study of the planets.

Around this time there were many other popular astrologers. One, John Gadbury, drew the retrospective birth charts of renowned, but dead people such as Nero, Henry VIII, Queen Elizabeth and Cardinal Richelieu. Another astrologer to make a wild claim was John Case, who calculated that the heavenly bodies had been created on Wednesday, 22nd April about 4002 years before Christ, Adam being created on the following day! In his work the *Angelical Guide*, published in 1697, Case suggests an astrologer may answer his clients' questions by putting certain queries to the appropriate signs. For instance, consult Sagittarius if somebody hopes to attain a high church office, or Libra to discover if he has a faithful wife, or Leo to find out if he would acquire for himself an agreeable girlfriend.

Before we drop the curtain on this motley crew, who seem to have very little in common with some of the previous learned stargazers, we might share a laugh with our eighteenth-century ancestors. A certain 'Isaac Bickerstaff' – in reality the great writer, Jonathan Swift, with his tongue in his cheek – published *Predictions for the year 1708*. In this he prophesied that John Partridge, an almanac maker who used his publications to emphasize his political and religious prejudices, would definitely die of fever at 11 p.m. on 29th March, and advised the astrologer to make all necessary preparations accordingly.

Nobody seemed to doubt this 'Bickerstaff'.

An astronomer making
calculations. Gradually
astronomy based on scientific
reasoning was replacing old
astrological ideas which relied
on tradition. Engraving by
Stradanus.

Page 110:
October. Page from a
manuscript of 'Les très riches
heures du Duc de Berry'
showing the rural scenes and
the signs of the zodiac
associated with that month.
Fifteenth-century French
manuscript. Musée Condé,
Chantilly.

Page 111:
November. Page from a
manuscript of 'Les très riches
heures du Duc de Berry'
showing the activities and
signs of the zodiac associated
with that month. Fifteenth-
century French manuscript.
Musée Condé, Chantilly.

Amused suspicion must have entered people's minds when 'Partridge'–in reality Jonathan Swift again–produced an attack on 'Bickerstaff's' prophesy. Poor Partridge probably deserves a little sympathy. He did not die until 1715, and had to advertise that not only was he alive but had been so on 29th March!

Astrology was no longer just a 'foolish daughter' of astronomy, but was rapidly becoming a rather shabby creature, and so we should not be too astonished to see it in decline in the next chapter.

Two 'hieroglyphics' by
William Lilly showing the
plague of 1665 and the Great
Fire of London the following
year, both events which he
claimed to have forecast nearly
twenty years previously.

111

Decline and Return

If astrology is regarded as some gloriously rampant blossom, then it was one which grew the seeds of its own blight. Men had gazed heavenwards for centuries, and had formulated a philosophy as to why the celestial bodies behaved in a particular way, but as time passed others made further observations and found disturbing facts which not only conflicted with, but made nonsense of, established ideas. At first, such theories and discoveries seemed pure blasphemy in the face of the sacrosanct teachings of Aristotle, Pythagoras and Ptolemy. The new seekers-after-truth began asking 'why?' in a rational rather than a mystical manner. The

Johann Kepler called astrology 'the foolish little daughter of the respectable reasonable mother astronomy'.

sixteenth-century wars of religion contributed to this questioning of accepted values which reached its peak during the eighteenth-century Age of Reason, when scientific knowledge shook superstition off its heels. The shock that upset the astrological applecart began as faint tremors in the sixteenth century.

The New Astronomers

Nicolas Copernicus (1473–1543) was virtually the father of modern astronomy, since it was his revolutionary theory which destroyed the Ptolemaic concept of a geocentric universe. Somehow this Polish doctor in canon law stumbled upon the truth that the earth and planets revolve around the sun. The idea was published posthumously in his *On the Revolution of the Celestial Orbs*. We cannot be sure how Copernicus viewed astrology, but his work was, paradoxically, pressed into its service by the German astronomer and mathematician known as Rheticus.

The Dane Tycho Brahe (1546–1601) was one of the first important observational (rather than theoretical) astronomers. He did not accept the heliocentric theory and, while he believed that stars influenced the individual's personality and life, he did not think very highly of astrologers. Notwithstanding, he drew birthcharts: perhaps for financial reasons or to please his friends.

Brahe's most outstanding astrological prediction arose from an event which shook Aristotelian theory to its foundations and gave weight to Copernican beliefs. In 1572 a comet appeared and Brahe forecast that, through its influence, a male child would be born in Finland in 1592, destined for a great career, who would die in religious strife in 1632. That great fighter for Protestantism, Gustavus Adolphus of Sweden, was actually born in 1594, and died at the Battle of Lützen in 1632. Finland was then part of Sweden, so that, apart from being two years out, Brahe's prophecy must be regarded with some respect.

By now we should not be surprised to learn that this comet was a source of inspiration to contemporary astrologers who made all sorts of predictions—mainly of the doom-laden variety—and concluded that among other things the new light in the sky heralded the end of the world or the Second Coming. What in fact it heralded was something momentous for astronomy. The comet was a 'nova'—a new star—

EFFIGIES TYCHONIS BRAHE O.F.
ÆDIFICII ET INSTRUMENTORUM
ASTRONOMICORUM STRUCTORIS.
Aº. DOMINI 1587, ÆTATIS SUÆ 40.

Nicolas Copernicus. His discovery that the earth and the planets revolved around the sun undermined traditional theories about astronomy and astrology. Berlin Observatory.

Tycho Brahe, in his observatory at Huen, was the first of the astronomers to observe rather than theorize.

Galileo Galilei, whose discovery of innumerable new stars did much to discredit astrological beliefs. Painting in the Biblioteca Marucelliana, Florence.

exploding in the constellation of Cassiopeia. Its appearance meant that the design of the constellations was not fixed but mutable, and therefore the Aristotelian concept of the fixed stars in the eighth sphere was disproved. Whether astrologers liked it or not the pattern of the stars could change.

It was Johann Kepler (1571–1630)–a curious blend of sceptic and mystic–who, as Brahe's assistant, worked on material already collected to become one of the prime architects of modern astronomy. Kepler termed astrology 'astronomy's foolish daughter', but nevertheless practised it–perhaps to help finance some of his research.

Neither the public nor the astrologers were ready to accept Kepler's highly individual and mystic views on astrology, for he wrote 'If I should express my own opinion it would be that there is no evil star in the heavens, chiefly for the following reasons: it is the nature of man as such . . . that lends to the planetary radiations their effect on itself; just as the sense of hearing, endowing with the faculty for discerning chords, lends to music such power that it incites him who hears it to dance.'

Kepler's predictions were of a political nature, including such events as an uprising among the Austrian peasantry in 1594 and the Austrian army's retreat from the Turks in 1595. It seems likely that his accuracy had more to do with his own astute mind and 'inside' court information than from the reading of signs in the skies. Whatever his beliefs about the more serious side of astrology, he despised what it had become at the popular level. Kepler produced astrological calendars which did not differ much from their astronomical counterparts. In 1598 he wrote about his latest calendar: 'As to all the prognoses I intend to present to my above-mentioned readers a pleasant enjoyment of the grandeur of nature along with the statements which appear true to me, thus hoping that the readers may be tempted to approve a raise in my salary. If you agree with this you will, I hope, not be angry with me, if as a defender of astrology in word and action, at the same time I try to implant the opinion in the masses that I am not an astrological buffoon . . .'

In 1610 Galileo (1564–1642) used the newly invented telescope, and with his own eyes destroyed another fundamental belief of traditional astrology. There were countless more fixed stars than anyone had ever imagined, and apparently four new planets–actually Jupiter's satellites. Such discoveries were not greeted enthusiastically by astrologers. Galileo, who was professor of mathematics at Pisa university, was actually imprisoned for proving the superiority of the Copernican over the Ptolemaic theory–such a discovery was regarded as heresy. However, whatever his personal feelings about astrology Galileo dabbled in it, but not very successfully.

The year Galileo died, Isaac Newton (1642–1727) was born in England. One feels that the mantle of astronomical observation must have fallen directly on to his shoulders. Copernicus, Kepler, and Galileo had prepared the way for Newton to demonstrate the theory of gravitation which showed that the universe was regulated by simple mathematical laws, and not mystical ones as had been previously believed. The English philosopher Francis Bacon (1561–1626), while not being an astronomer, helped to lay the foundation for Newton's mode of reasoning when he set aside Aristotelian deductive logic in favour of the inductive method. His writings were instrumental in bringing about the creation of the Royal Society in 1662.

Sir Isaac Newton. His theory of gravitation showed that the universe was ruled by simple mathematical laws rather than supernatural ones. National Portrait Gallery, London.

Despite all these reasonable and reasoning minds, when the famous comet appeared in 1680 a cultured man like the diarist John Evelyn could still wonder if it might be a warning from God. This particular comet was greeted in various ways, demonstrating how different societies reacted to a phenomenon which would once have caused general awe, consternation and much studying of horoscopes. In Germany, educated and religious men declared that the length of the comet's tail was a sign of God's wrath. The attitude of the sophisticated French was more phlegmatic. The playwright, Bernard Fontenelle, wrote a satirical comedy, 'La Comète', in 1681, which mocked astrologers and the comet. The attack by the philosopher, Pierre Bayle, on astrology was provoked as much by the comet as by the multitude of French astrologers. Like many astronomers he correctly guessed that comets might be periodic, which basically undermined the whole idea of the comet of great portent. In America the preacher, Increase Mather saw the comet as a heaven-sent opportunity for delivering a series of puritanical sermons to his flock on the imminent wrath of God. 'As for the sign in heaven now appearing, what calamities may be portended thereby? . . . In general we have cause to fear that sweeping judgements are thereby signified; that the Lord is coming down from Heaven with a long beesom of destruction which shall sweep away a world of sinners before it . . .' How he and his congregation coped with the anticlimax, when there was no flood or holocaust, it is hard to imagine.

It is difficult for people in our age, daily bombarded by new and often incomprehensible scientific discoveries, to understand the consternation caused by the finding of new planets. In 1781 the English astronomer William Herschel discovered Uranus, which he tried to call Georgium Sidus after King George III. Out of loyalty his friends wanted it to be called Herschel, but although this name may be found in some old grammars of astrology, the classical tradition prevailed and the newly found planet was given a Roman god's name to match those of its heavenly cousins. At first astrologers ignored this new arrival and stuck grimly to the planets everyone knew. Eventually Uranus was declared to be the ruler of Aquarius. Not surprisingly, new planets became associated with events or inventions occurring after their discovery. Uranus was linked with the dawn of the Industrial Revolution and machinery.

In 1846 the even more distant Neptune was discovered by the French astronomer, Urbain Leverrier. Since the god Neptune is traditionally the guardian of the oceans, astrologers chose to connect this planet with the sea, and made it rule over Pisces.

In 1930 Pluto was discovered by Percival Lowell. Astrologers are still not fully agreed about Pluto's precise functions, but some relate it to Aries, and see its influence as malign, especially in connection with the age of nuclear weapons.

During the Age of Reason devotees of astrology – particularly in England – were trying

THE Sun now shines upon the Lion bold,

Leo, with fiery eye, and shaggy mane;

See, midst the hay, the merry children rolled,

While all around, hay harvest strews the plain.

An illustration and a rhyme about the signs of the zodiac and the seasons they control from a nineteenth-century children's book. In the possession of Zodiac, The Astrological Emporium, London.

Urbain Jean Joseph Leverrier, the French astronomer whose researches indicated the existence of the planet Neptune, which was later proved by telescopic search. From 'Astronomie Populaire' (1880).

to keep the belief in it alive. William Derham, a fellow of the Royal Society and a clergyman, wrote *Astro Theology*, which proved very popular. The physician, Ebenezer Sibly, who described himself as an 'astro-philosopher' compiled the voluminous *A New and Complete illustration of the Celestial Science of Astrology* which contained among other things a collection of nativities. One of its imaginative illustrations symbolized the American Revolution, and showed a horoscope cast for the Declaration of Independence in 1776. It was, however, produced some eight years after the event. Other astrologers had little love for Sibly, and declared him a quack who stole other men's writings. What he actually did was to garner material from older astrological works, which preserved them for posterity.

To demonstrate his skills another astrological writer, John Worsdale, collected a selection of his own predictions in the *Celestial Philosophy*. He was a regular Cassandra since most of these prophecies were of the unfortunate kind. When young Mary Dickson asked him about the date of her wedding Worsdale replied lugubriously: 'I was confident she would never enter into the matrimonial union. She said she was sorry I should give false judgement as she expected to marry in the ensuing Spring. I then informed her that something of an awful nature would occur before the month of March . . . which would destroy life.' Drowning was to be poor Mary's fate. Despite her prophet's repeated warnings against such an action she travelled by water and was drowned. We have no proof, however, whether the prediction was made before or after the event!

By the later eighteenth century astrology's reputation was very suspect indeed. Beyond Europe, of course, astrology continued to cast its spell as it had done for centuries. In India, Persia, and Egypt English travellers saw people's lives swayed by the dictates of the planets—perhaps this gave the European rationalists a sense of superiority in that they were no longer subject to the superstition governing non-Christians.

The Persistence of Belief

Yet all this scientific rationalism produced a reaction among a cultivated minority, in rather the same way as our own technological age is witnessing a resurgence of interest in matters paranormal. During the nineteenth century

America

Independance

4th July 10H

10m P.M

1776

cabbalistic numerology, medieval magic, and astrology became mixed up together. In 1855 Alphonse Louis Constant, the French occultist (better known under his penname of Eliphas Levi), quoted in his *History of Magic*: 'Astrology is a synthesis because the Tree of Life is a single tree and because its branches–spread through heaven and bearing flowers of stars–are in correspondence with its roots, which are hidden in earth.'

The labours of these nineteenth-century cabbalists were adapted for less esoteric purposes by later astrologers: the mystical science of numbers in conjunction with planetary lore was employed to provide racing and share tips.

The famous Zadkiel, in his *Handbook of Astrology*, explains rather pompously that he regretted anyone exploiting astrology to pursue this 'pernicious, foolish and discreditable practice for the sake of mammon', but his book was intended to be of service in allaying the worries

of those who gambled. A curious splitting of hairs–do not use astrology to find the winner for gain but to prevent you from worrying about the result!

Despite the Witchcraft and Vagrancy Acts–mainly directed at back-street astrologers and gypsies–the appetite for astrology of the mass of the English people was to be catered for by a host of popular astrologers. The disapproval expressed in serious newspapers and periodicals had little effect on the wide readership of cheap pamphlets, which may not have been exactly original but were certainly copious.

An extract from an almanac for 1820 shows us the sort of thing to be found in ordinary homes or in the servants' quarters below stairs. Such publications might also include the coach time-table for that area, a list of local officials and justices of the peace, details of stamp and other duties, and market days.

'I begin the New Year with this Quarter, as it

all falls within the quarter, excepting a few days. This Quarter then takes place when the Sun enters Capricorn, the Southern Solstice, which according to my calculations he will do on Wednesday the 22nd December 1819, at 5 minutes past 3 o'clock in the afternoon. They who please to erect a scheme of the Heavens, adapted to the above time, will find 20 degrees of Gemini ascending in the East and 14 degrees of Aquarius passing the Meridian or culminating. At this time the Moon is applying to a Sextile aspect of the Planet Venus, and next hastening to a conjunction of the Planet Saturn; at this time there is also a conjunction of the Planet Saturn; at this time there is also a conjunction of the Sun and Mercury both going down in the western quarter and angular; the Planet Jupiter is also angular and full South; all the Planets are above the Earth, excepting the Planet Mars, who is positioned in the 3rd House of the Figure, moving retrograde; the Moon and Saturn are positioned in the 11th House, and Venus was following the Sun in the West. After this manner are all the Planets distributed in the Heavens at this Ingress. From these Configurations of the Planets, I expect in this Quarter many deliberate councils and deep consultations in the Cabinets of the Mighty, especially more so in the Spring. The Parliament of England will soon meet, when some great proceedings will be brought before them. I wish it may end for the good and satisfaction of the People of the British nation. The most material configurations of this Quarter do give hopes, and imply a continuance of Peace in the European Kingdoms. God grant Peace and Tranquility may still be continued amongst them. The affairs of Spain will be much disturbed, especially more in the Spring, with internal Broils, dissatisfaction and contention; and the Emperor of Russia is still very active in improving his Country. As to the Weather, I fear in many places infirmities and bodily distempers will be too much abound; yet although there may be shrewd conjectures for the particular month from the Sun's ingress into Capricorn, to his advent in Aries, yet nothing that carries the bold face of infallibility is at all warrantable; since the

Title page from 'The Astrologer of the Nineteenth Century' (London, 1825).

A hieroglyphic of the signs of heaven at the eclipse of the moon, 3 November, 1827, from 'Raphael's Astrological Allegory' (1827).

state of the air is not uniform in all places in the same kingdom, province, or even country; but is strangely different in regard to the difference of weather in various Places at the same time; from which cause likewise experience has long since determined one part of a nation to be the sea of Health, while another is found to be the parent of Agues and various other disorders. . . .'

Stripped of their high-flown planetary vocabulary the predictions are very scant indeed, and nobody could pin down this prophet to a definite weather forecast.

The astrologers who sold their services to an ever-widening English audience were a curiously mixed bunch, who masked their more prosaic names under the titles of Hebrew angels. Sepharial, Raphael, Aphorel and Zadkiel imparted a mystic respectability to their predictions and manuals. One of the chief features of nineteenth-century astrology was that it ceased to be a purely private matter between 'native' (the person for whom a horoscope is drawn) and astrologer. Now ordinary people could read their own stars in numerous publications and even learn to produce their own birth charts.

The first Zadkiel was the sort of eccentric who seems to abound among the English middle classes. His real name was Richard James Morrison, and he was a half-pay lieutenant in the Royal Navy. He resigned from the service to devote the next sixty years to astrology and inventions of various kinds. Well-educated and widely read in obscure subjects, Morrison was also a skilful and colourful writer who would have been successful in a better genre of

Astrology has always been a popular subject for artists. A young student of the ancient science, as seen by the seventeenth-century Dutch painter, Franz van Mieris. National Gallery, London.

journalism had he not seen the resurrection of the reputation of astrology as a kind of cause.

For Zadkiel astrology was a branch of the occult, and he also indulged in crystal-gazing—even publishing the information received from the 'other world' in his famous almanac. Zadkiel's almanacs were highly popular, and sold 60,000 copies annually. Before the outbreak of the First World War the circulation had risen to 200,000. Morrison also produced a *Grammar of Astrology*, and reintroduced the works of William Lilly to an eager public. After censuring various English astrologers including Lilly, Sibly, and Gadbury in his introduction to the *Grammar of Astrology* because they 'were immersed in error when they treated on nativities', Zadkiel goes on to recommend his own work because 'In short, there exists no

brief, cheap, elementary work on the science, except the *Grammar of Astrology*. It contains nothing that is not founded on actual experience. The author then explains that the *Grammar of Astrology* is intended to teach the principles of the science of nativities and to render them so plain, by divesting them of the trash which designing or ignorant men have introduced, that persons of an ordinary capacity and a common share of industry may examine and decide for themselves whether there be any truth in astrology or not. . . .'

He concluded with dubious humility 'In perfect but humble confidence in the purity of his intentions in endeavouring to gain a hearing for Astrology, the Author can contemplate with perfect calm the bitterness of abuse of some men who call themselves, par excellence, philos-

The 'Mystical Wheel of Pythagoras', used in numerical divination, from 'Raphael's Witch or The Oracle of the Future' (1831).

ophers; since he finds, by the steady sale of the first edition of this book and the numerous other similar publications he has brought before the public, that there are many who will soar above prejudice and resolve on seeing with their own eyes.'

Morrison was obviously sincere about astrology, although it did not prevent him finding it lucrative. He charged up to £10 for a private sitting, and this probably went a long way towards convincing his clients that they were getting genuine value for their money. During the 1840s and the early 1850s a number of astrologers were arrested, and Zadkiel tried in vain to get the Vagrancy Act of 1824 altered. This had made fortune-telling by the stars a punishable offence.

In his 1861 *Almanac* he predicted the death of Prince Albert. The accuracy of this forecast provoked the unflattering attention of the press. The *Daily Telegraph* sneered: 'Once in every five years one of Zadkiel's prophecies, which are generally the stupidest jumping at probable eventualities, may by an accident come true. Whereupon the seer goes into raptures of the ''Right Again!'' description, and sells his almanacs, we are sorry to learn, by the thousand! . . . We might pass this rubbishing pamphlet by with contempt, but the publicity it has recently attained demands that it and its author should be exposed and denounced. The one is a sham, the other is a swindler.'

After this a rear admiral in the Royal Navy informed the *Daily Telegraph* that Lieutenant Morrison had not served in the navy for forty-seven years, and furthermore 'A friend of mine reminds me that the author of Zadkiel is the celebrated crystal globe seer who gulled many of our nobility about the year 1852. Making use of a boy under fourteen or a girl under twelve, he pretended by their looking into the crystal globe, to hold converse with the spirits of the

Jupiter rules the destinies of the great, and in ancient times the astrologer calculated the influences shed by its light. From 'Astronomie Populaire' (1880).

THE DESTRUCTION OF POMPEII.

THE ENCHANTRESS OF THE WATERS.

Apostles–even our Saviour, with all the angels of light as well as darkness, and to tell what was going on in any part of the world. One noble lady gave the boy £5 to give her intelligence regarding her boy, who was in the Mediterranean. . . .'

A libel case ensued. An astrologer's honour was not regarded too highly: for Zadkiel was awarded twenty shillings damages but no costs. However, this did not affect the sale of his almanacs. (You can read some of Zadkiel's descriptions of the effects of zodiac and planets in the last chapter.)

Morrison was a member of the Mercurii–the first astrological society to be established since the seventeenth century. Its probable founder was Robert Cross Smith, who came to London from Bristol in 1820 to make his living as a hack in astrological journalism. Smith, who was totally different in background and outlook from Morrison, edited various astrological works, but his real success was the popular *Raphael's Almanac*, which flourished under that name long after its originator was dead. Raphael's *Witch* was illustrated with such choice items as the 'Mystical Wheel of Pythagoras' and the 'Cabbalistical Tablet of the Stars'.

Here is a 'singular prediction of the astrologer Raphael'. 'In the month of August, 1822, a lady was introduced to this gentleman, by means of a friend, and requested to know the events which were pending at that period. The artist drew forth the horoscope, and informed her that, from the position of heavenly bodies at that instant, he foresaw she would be in danger of "taking poison", through the carelessness of a servant, and therefore warned her to be very careful what medicine she took for the next six months. The prediction was thought but little of at the time, but within six months from that period, the astrologer received a letter in the lady's own handwriting, stating "that the cup was actually raised to her lips, when recollecting the injunction, she was induced to examine it, and discovered it to be poison, delivered by the servant in mistake," as was foretold. A striking proof of the science.'

To make matters more confusing there were about six different writers using the name 'Raphael' between 1820 and 1850, editing such works as *The Philosophical Merlin*, *The Astrologer of the 19th Century*, *Urania*, *Familiar Astrology*, *Raphael's Sanctuary of the Astral Art*, and *The Prophetic Art*. Some of the chapters to be found in these books deal with other aspects of the occult, such as necromancy, charms, talismans and terrifying legends, as well as horoscopes and the grammar of astrology, rather as today's astrological magazines contain articles on seances, ghosts, etc. Although Zadkiel started publishing astronomical ephemerides, these later appeared under Raphael's name.

The third editor of *Zadkiel's Almanac* was A. J. Pearce, who was especially interested in associating diseases with planetary influences, and was the author of a book about astrology and its relationship to the diagnosis and treatment of disease. Writing in the 1840s, William Joseph Simmonites dealt with herbal cures and their links with traditional astrology, and in the final chapter you can read some prescriptions for staying healthy according to your sun sign.

Shewing the Effects of the Planets, and other Astronomical Constellations.

With the strange Events that befall Men, Women, and Children, born under them.

Compiled by, *GODFRIDUS*, *super palladium de Agricultura Anglicarum*.

Together with the Husbandmans Practice: Or, Prognostication for ever; as teacheth *Albert*, *Alkind*, and *Ptolomy*.

With the Shepherds Prognostication for the weather, and *Pythagoras* his Wheel of Fortune.

This is unknown to many Men, Though it be known to some Men.

Printed for *W. Thackeray*, and are to be sold at his Shop, at the Angel in Duck-Lane, 1679.

The kind of work popular among ordinary folk in the seventeenth century: a mixture of star lore, superstition and agricultural tips, given respectability by the mention of Ptolemy and Pythagoras.

This new breed of nineteenth-century astrologers was not allowed to go unchallenged. In 1838 a professor of mathematics, T. H. Moody, published a *Complete Refutation of Astrology*. Besides criticizing certain of Zadkiel's predictions and theories Moody described the pathetic malpractices of unscrupulous astrological charlatans. He also poured scorn on the links between astrology and science and mathematics. It is doubtful whether Moody's attack made much impression upon an audience already addicted to books and pamphlets promising to give them a glimpse into the future.

The nineteenth century also witnessed the blending of biblical symbolism and mysticism with regular astrology. In 1862 Frances Rolleston published *Mazzaroth* (the Hebrew for 'zodiac'), in which she explained the zodiacal references she had unearthed in the Bible. Karl Anderson, who called himself a professor of Chaldean, Arabian, and Egyptian astrology, published *Astrology of the Old Testament*, which was a mystical fusion of astrology and Freemasonry, and linked the zodiac with the Twelve Tribes of Israel.

About this time the astrologer Rosa Baugham used her own version of the wheel of Pythagoras to make predictions by numbers based on questions put by her clients. Her brand of astrology smacks very much of the macrocosm and microcosm, for she claimed that each planet ruled a particular finger and a facial line.

In 1875 Madame Helena Blavatsky founded the Theosophical Society in New York, and became instrumental in giving astrology the accolade of respectability. Theosophy turned from traditional Western religious thought to embrace the mystical doctrines of the East, particularly India, which led back to the idea of viewing the stars as divinities who were the 'cause' rather than the 'sign' of events. Madame Blavatsky wrote confidently: 'Why see in the Pisces a direct reference to Christ—one of the several world reformers, a saviour but for his direct followers, but only a great and glorious Initiate for all the rest—when that constellation shines as a symbol of all the past, present, and future Spiritual Saviours who dispense light and dispel mental darkness?'

'The Hierographical Prediction of the Death of the Late King of France' by Raphael. This was said to have been sent to the engraver some months before the king actually died. From 'The Astrologer of the Nineteenth Century' (London, 1825).

Tablet of Questions and the
Cabbalistical Tablet of the
Stars from 'Raphael's Witch or
the Oracle of the Future' (1831).

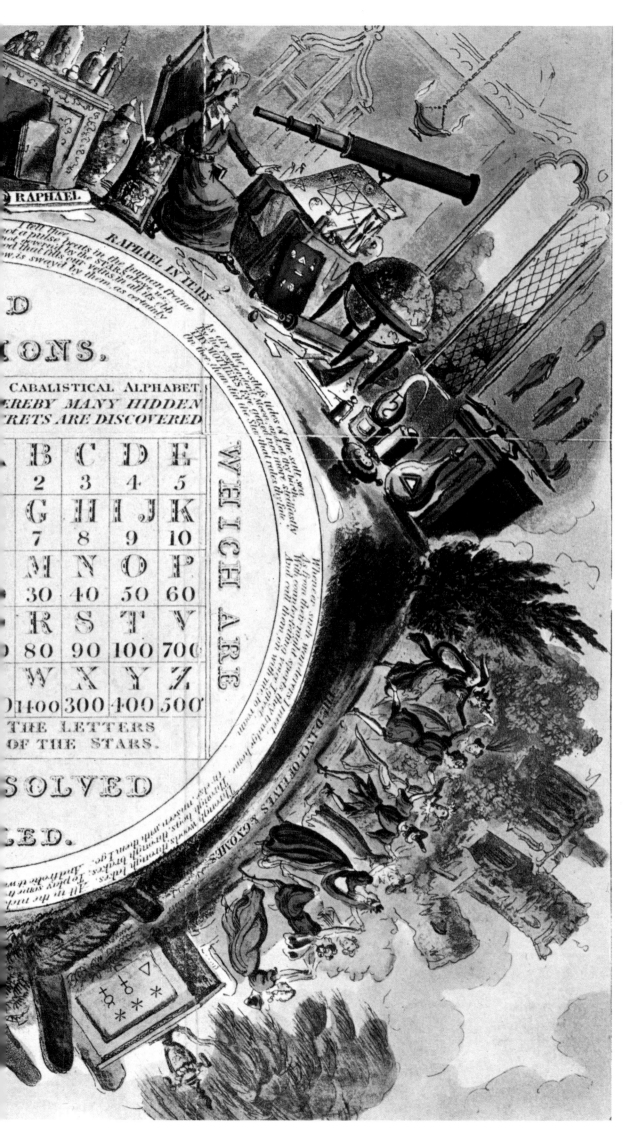

Right:
Urania—the muse of astronomy —weighing the system of the world. Fascimile of an engraving of 1651. From 'Astronomie Populaire' (1880).

Far right:
Mars presiding over the slaughter at Thermopylae. From 'Astronomie Populaire' (1880).

Annie Besant, photographed in 1885, became president of the Theosophical Society in succession to Madame Blavatsky.

Through its lively propaganda and display of arcane wisdom Theosophy became socially acceptable. Since it had none of the grubby fairground associations of quack magicians, it gave astrology an introduction into the polite drawing rooms, and allowed all sorts of highly respected and educated people to re-examine the subject. In her difficult work *The Secret Doctrine* Madame Blavatsky says positively: 'Yes, our destiny is written in the stars! . . . This is not superstition, least of all is it fatalism. . . . It is now amply proved that even horoscopes and judiciary astrology are not quite based on fiction, and that Stars and Constellations, consequently, have an occult and mysterious influence on, and connection with, individuals. And if with the latter, why not with nations, races, and mankind as a whole?'

Even the perplexing problem of the new planets which traditional astrologers had done their utmost to ignore was dealt with by the redoubtable Madame Blavatsky. Theosophy accepted the proposition put forward by Indian astrology that each sign of the zodiac had a separate planetary ruler—so why should more planets not be discovered?

Her successor as president of the Theosophical Society was Annie Besant, who had less extreme views on astrology, and admitted she knew little about the subject. She wrote: 'At the most, astrology, as it is now practised can only calculate the interaction between these physical conditions at any given moment, and the conditions brought to them by a given person whose general constitution and natal conditions are known. It cannot say what the person will do, nor what will happen to them. . . .' She also felt it was important to examine the person's character as well as the horoscope.

Astrology had once more attained such a degree of respectability in England that a man like Richard Garnett (1835–1900), Keeper of Printed Books in the British Museum, could openly claim to believe in astrology while dismissing its occult and mystical connections. He thought it should be the most exacting of sciences since it depended so much on precise mathematical calculations, and saw it as an aid to assessing the human character rather than predicting the future. This was fundamentally an attempt to link astrology with psychology.

However, the father of psychology, Sigmund

Freud, was only marginally interested in the subject through his friend and colleague Wilhelm Fleiss, who sought a relationship between the behaviour of planets and the body's rhythm. He found nothing to convince Freud on the efficacy of astrology. Another Theosophical astrologer was William Allen (known as Alan Leo). Leo believed 'that every man derives his will power from a Planetary Sphere of Influences which he uses or abuses, by which he can overcome evil tendencies, and control his animal nature, hence Astrology teaches that Character is Destiny, also that the Wise Man rules his Stars while the fool obeys them.'

All sorts of people took Leo seriously, including bankers who helped finance him and Aphorel (F. W. Lacey) to publish the *Astrological Magazine* in 1890. In 1895 they renamed their publication *Modern Astrology*. This flourished greatly, for it offered its readers the opportunity of paying one shilling to get his or her own personal horoscope. Such a device was so popular that Leo had to employ a temporary staff of astrologers to cope with the demand. Between 1900 and 1903 the birthcharts alone made £1000 clear profit (worth £10,000 nowadays.).

After 1903 the mass horoscopes ceased, but Leo still drew individual nativities, and published astrological literature designed to enable people to learn how to draw their own birth charts. This did not put the professional astrologers out of business; if anything, it fanned popular interest.

Leo married a Theosophist, Bessie, on her condition that the union should remain unconsummated. It seems their marriage was indeed made in heaven—or the sky—for such a union was considered a good idea, since their horo-

Illustration from Eliphas Levi's 'History of Magic', personifying the seven planets. Levi was one of the nineteenth-century occultists who strove to keep interest in astrology alive.

scopes showed his sun and her moon to be in the same degree of Aries. Leo taught Bessie astrology and allowed her to write for his magazine.

Another Theosophist and astrologer was Dr W. Gorn-Old known as Sepharial. Like Alan Leo he was interested in Hindu astrology as well as the traditional Western kind, and also in magic, Cabbalism, and numerology. Sepharial must have had a pretty realistic streak, too, for just before the First World War he published *The Silver Key*, an astrological handbook to horse-

A Talisman for Love. This is said to be wonderfully useful in obtaining success in love adventures. It must be made in the day and hour of Venus, when she is favourable to the planet Mars. It should be made in pure silver, or purified copper. If Venus is in the sign of Taurus or Libra (her particular houses) this is even better. From 'The Astrologer of the Nineteenth Century' (London, 1825).

Right:
Percival Lowell, 1855–1916, the American astronomer who was the first to deduce the existence of the planet Pluto, discovered in 1930.

Far right:
The extraordinary Madame Blavatsky, founder of the Theosophical Society in New York and author of 'The Secret Doctrine'.

Right:
Richard Garnett, Keeper of the Printed Books in the British Museum, saw astrology as a science. National Portrait Gallery, London.

Far right:
John Evans, the ill-favoured astrologer of Wales. By the late eighteenth century astrologers were beginning to lose their aura of respectability and authority and become figures of fun. Engraving.

Opposite page:
Mid-Victorian zodiacal cards. Prints kindly lent by the Baynton-Williams Gallery, Belgravia, London.

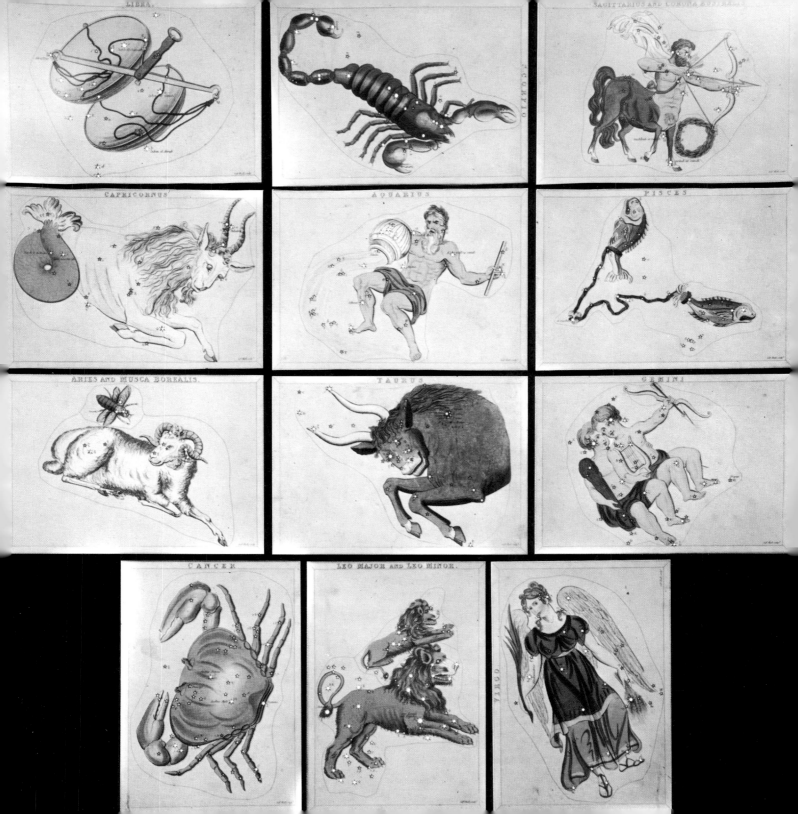

racing, linking colours and names with the planets. He achieved some spectacular successes in forecasting the winners of races, but his attempt to predict the date of Annie Besant's death was less fortunate: she actually lived twenty-six years longer than his forecast.

In the *Great Devastation* (c. 1914) Sepharial explained that a reference to the war could be found in chapter 11 of the Book of Daniel, provided Germany was substituted for Persia and France for Greece.

In 1908 *Old Moore's Almanac* had done better than that, for it warned the British public that: 'The Kaiser's Ascendant is nearly opposite the Mars of King Edward of England, while Mercury is on Mars in the latter, a certain indication of disputes and quarrels, and that natural action of the latter is likely to militate against the former's colonial policy. We call special attention to the point, because in view of the coming planetary influences and especially eclipses there is no doubt that the dogs of war cannot be held in the leash much longer. . . .'

Sepharial's cheery forecast must have seemed rather incongruous during that grim time when he wrote: 'We are about to enter upon the Aquarian Age wherein Humanity will be its own Dictator, when the public conscience shall be a law unto itself, and the service of Goodwill shall become the sweet slavery of the Soul.' Wishful thinking indeed when we recall the horrors of trench warfare.

In 1915 Sepharial optimistically published *Why the War Will End in 1917*. He predicted 'an Aquarian Age of a liberated humanity . . . marked by beneficent Communism.' The millennium would occur in 2449, but before that there was to be 'the great climacteric, which lasts from 1991 to 1997, and which ensanguines the whole of the East . . .'

Astrologers like Sepharial and Leo did a flourishing trade during the war, patriotically predicting victories. In fact, during all national crises, the horoscope casters provided a fillip to morale by pointing out the good aspects of their own country's stars, and the malign ones of those of the enemy's leader, be he Napoleon or Hitler.

'Libra—Striking the Balance.' One of a number of book illustrations by George Cruikshank mocking the signs of the zodiac. In the possession of Zodiac, The Astrological Emporium, London.

133

The Twentieth Century

Opposite page:
Mandala drawn by C. G. Jung.
This symbol represents the
totality of all things in the
universe. Of astrology the
Swiss psychologist wrote:
'From the scientific point of
view there is little hope of
proving that astrological
correspondence is something
that conforms to law'.

Evangeline Adams, the
American astrologer, who
wrote her own horoscope: 'I
have Mars conjunct my natal
Sun in the twelfth House. I will
always triumph over my
enemies'.

The Controversy Continues

Many readers may perhaps feel that the twentieth century can hardly warrant a chapter to
itself, for surely by now astrology wields its
power only at the popular level – people following their 'stars' in the paper, wearing a zodiac
charm, buying astrologically associated notions
(anything from tea-towels to T-shirts) or simply
saying 'I'm a Leo, you're a Sagittarius, so we
must hit it off'. In fact, astrology – that ancient
'chimera' – however battered, abused and
bloody, is still alive, unbowed, and kicking. Its
antagonists are just as scathing as in previous
ages – even more so, armed as they are with a
battery of hard scientific knowledge.

Robert Eisler, one of astrology's severest
critics, in his *The Royal Art of Astrology* (published 1946) wrote about modern defenders of
astrology: 'They will not acknowledge honestly
the decisive fact that their futile practices have
been investigated with the greatest care and
impartiality by the foremost scholars of the
leading Western nations for now almost three
centuries, and that not one of these has failed to
condemn them as the stale, superstitious residue
of what was once a great, pantheistic religion
and a glorious philosophical attempt to understand and rationally to explain the universe, a
bold enterprise to which we owe not only the
whole of our astronomical knowledge, but the
most essential part of all our physical science.'

His scorn at particular constellations providing definite influences was boundless when he
dealt with our old friend the 'precession of
equinoxes'. However, most modern astrologers get round this by declaring that such
stars are 'signs' rather than 'causes'.

On the other hand astrology's adherents are
just as mixed a bunch as in earlier times. Some
are as convinced and serious as the Chaldean
priests, others as dubious as any of the astrologers to be found in the seventeenth century,
and of course there are the genuine scientists who
have been experimenting in an attempt to
discover exactly what influences may reach
our planet from the heavens.

While the Church is not very keen on astrology, nowadays nobody gets burnt at the stake
for practising it. However, the civil authorities
are not always lenient, and even in this century
a number of serious-minded astrologers have
been prosecuted under the Vagrancy Law for
following their profession.

In 1917, Alan Leo was fined £5 with £25 costs
for 'pretending and professing to tell fortunes'.
He had already been prosecuted once, in 1914,
but the case had been dismissed. On this
occasion the judge remained unmoved by the
defence which claimed Leo was only practising
something in which he firmly believed, and
that his clients were drawn from the educated
and wealthy. Nor was the judge impressed by
the fact that Leo was one of the Committee in the
Society for Astrological Research, which still
exists as the Astrological Lodge of the Theosophical Society.

However, it was in the United States – where
astrology had not yet gained a foothold – that a
court case took place which put astrology back

135

on the map. The defendant was a woman, Mrs George E. Jordan, known better as Evangeline Adams (1865–1932). According to what she herself said: 'I have Mars conjunct my natal Sun in the twelfth House. I will always triumph over my enemies.' She certainly did, and became the best-known astrologer in the United States, so much so that her funeral had the trappings associated with the death of a Hollywood star.

This remarkable woman gave astrology to the masses, and was instrumental in promoting the annual American demand for millions of horoscopes, and therefore for giving later astrologers a chance to make a prosperous living.

In 1914 Evangeline Adams was charged with fortune-telling. She conducted her own defence, produced all the books of reference she used in charting a horoscope, and then proceeded to draw one for a complete stranger–in fact, the judge's own son. The judge was impressed enough to decide 'the defendant raises astrology to the dignity of an exact science,' and the case was dismissed. In New York astrology ceased to be thought of as fortune-telling, which, as is the case in England, is outside the law.

In 1936 in England, after the star columns had caught the public's interest, R. H. Naylor, who made predictions for the *Sunday Express*, found himself the target of the editor of the *Psychic News* who 'laid information' that Naylor was contravening the Vagrancy Act by 'pretending to read fortunes'. The editor was not a disinterested party: mediums were penalized under the Witchcraft Act and did not see why the astrologers should escape legal sanctions. Eventually, the case reached the Lord Chief Justice and other Lords of Appeal, who apparently looked on star columns in a rather lighthearted way. Perhaps the spiritualists ought to have consulted the astrologers before having recourse to law, for they lost a costly case!

The Vagrancy Act is still in force, and now and again the police will prosecute itinerant fortune-tellers and crystalgazers, but for the most part newspaper and professional astrologers go unmolested by the law.

The career of Evangeline Adams is the stuff of popular novels. When she first arrived in New York to stay at the Windsor Hotel on Fifth Avenue, she examined the owner's birth chart and then warned him that in it she read imminent catastrophe. The following day the hotel burnt down. Among her clients were such

Louis de Wohl, the Hungarian-born astrologer, who worked for the British Government during the Second World War. Of astrology he wrote '. . . it is not prophecy. It is dealing not with certainties but with tendencies. It has a fairly wide margin for error . . . but it works . . .'

The American writer, Henry Miller, who wrote of astrology 'What it does . . . is to show us there is a correspondence between macrocosm and microcosm . . . Whether astrology be a science or a pseudo-science, the fact remains that the oldest and the greatest civilizations we know of had for centuries upon centuries used it as a basis for thought and action . . .'

R. H. Naylor, the initiator of the twentieth-century star column in the daily press, speaking at a Foyles literary luncheon in November 1941.

famous people as Enrico Caruso, Mary Pickford and the millionaire, J. P. Morgan, to whom she gave financial advice as dictated by the stars. Even nowadays many wealthy and successful men, who we might think of as too hard-headed and materialistic to consult anyone other than stockbrokers, tax experts and the like, go to astrologers for advice on the hazards of life, both business and personal. However, it is impossible to avoid the conclusion that if astrologers were so adept at predicting the movements of shares they would make enough money on their own account to retire. In 1930 Evangeline Adams had her own radio programme and therefore a nationwide audience to whom she gave advice and predictions.

In 1928 the American Federation of Astrologers was founded with the intention of disassociating astrology from the mumbo-jumbo of magic, and making it thoroughly reputable. Registered with this organization are over 1500 astrologers, and in the United States there are more than 5000 practising astrologers, with more than 10,000,000 clients, from every stratum of society. Both in America and elsewhere there are many astrological societies – some of impeccable reputation, others less so.

The Faculty of Astrological Studies (associated with the previously mentioned Astrological Lodge) was established in London in 1948. If you want to get 'D.F. Astrol. S' after your name you have to study for three years and take examinations. There is no doubt that the Faculty and its students take their work very seriously, and to free it from any imputation of charlatanism the following tenets must be upheld:

'I will undertake no natal work unless the time and place of birth are stated with reasonable accuracy, or if these are not available, I will explain clearly and unequivocally that any work supplied in such circumstances can only be regarded as inadequate and general.

'In all professional work I will charge a fee commensurate with the dignity of astrological science, except in cases wherein the inquirer, being a genuine seeker after help and not impelled by idle curiosity, is unable to make a payment. In such instances I will give information and advice gratuitously.

'I will in every case make an original and individual study of the case before me and will not use any form of reduplication, nor will I use in my work extracts from others' writings without due acknowledgement.

'In work stated to be astrological I will not insert anything that is not founded upon true astrological science. Should I desire to impart advice for information derived from other sources I will write this upon a separate sheet with an express statement that it is not based upon Astrology.

'I agree to respect in the strictest manner all confidences reposed in me, unless my duty as a loyal and law-abiding citizen of my country compels me to act otherwise.

'I will use discretion in making any public statements regarding political matters or persons prominent in public life, and will avoid all such as are contrary to good taste and the practice of a decent reticence.

'I undertake to make no improper or unethical use of the Diploma and my status as a Holder thereof and a Member of the Faculty; and as far as in me lies I will conduct all professional astrological work, should I be engaged therein, in accordance with high professional standards.

'I will hold for the general good and not for my private use or advantage any discoveries that I may make or conclusions that I may reach, save only such as might, if divulged in public, conduce to results undesirable in the general interest.'

In the United Kingdom you may spend anything between £2 and £50 on consulting an astrologer – but do remember galloping inflation – and most of these, through the vigilance of the reputable astrological bodies, may be considered ethical, whether or not they cast horoscopes for individual clients or write star columns for the press. However, nobody should be surprised that there are also quacks whose horoscopes are not the work of study and calculation, but merely 'made up' – occasionally differing little from the manufactured item you obtain by putting a coin in a slot machine.

A real twentieth-century innovation is the computerized horoscope – if any kind of data can be fed into one of these machines, why not that pertaining to the stars? What it lacks in the personal touch, it certainly makes up for in length of results. The wealth of detail fed into such a machine does mean that among the verbose horoscopes it churns out will be some fairly accurate character readings!

Let us leave machines and return to individuals. Hardly in the Evangeline Adams' class was the Dane, Max Heindel, who seems to have been attracted by the remunerative as well as the mystical aspect of astrology. Influenced by Rudolph Steiner's breakaway Theosophy sect in Berlin, Heindel moved to the United States, where he joined the Universal Brotherhood – another Theosophy splinter group – and then left to found his own occult society, the Rosi-crucian Fellowship, in San Francisco. His disciples were conducted through the mysteries of the arcane world by 'Master's Letters' garnered from material taken from Steiner's lectures. It seems doubtful whether Heindel made any successful predictions, but he wrote a considerable amount about astrology, and his 'Message of the Stars' was particularly popular – although inaccurate. Among Heindel's theories are these: that surgery should preferably be performed during a waxing moon, that cardinal signs help with curing an invalid whereas the fixed ones prove intransigent, and that Neptune 'does not really belong in our solar system . . .' – rather it is 'The embodiment of a Great Spirit from the Creative Hierarchies which normally influence us from the Zodiac.'

In the 1930s astrology enjoyed a remarkable revival in Europe. On the 24th August, 1930, the *Sunday Express* printed the horoscope of Margaret Rose, the second daughter of the Duke and Duchess of York, who had been born three days previously. The astrologer was R. H. Naylor who might be regarded as the initiator of twentieth-century newspaper mundane astrology. Royalty and prophesy are a heady mixture for public consumption. In October Naylor predicted some catastrophe associated with a British aircraft *before* the destruction of the airship R.101. The newspaper star columns were thoroughly launched. No popular Sunday or daily was complete without its astrologer, who, naturally,

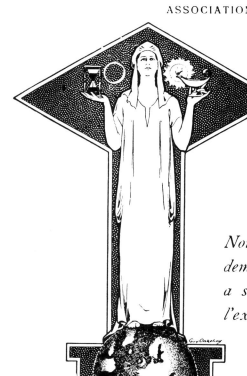

INSTITUT CENTRAL BELGE DE RECHERCHES ASTRO-DYNAMIQUES

ASSOCIATION SANS BUT LUCRATIF, FONDÉE EN 1926

Cours public d'Astrologie Scientifique

DEGRÉ

(1ᵉʳ DEGRÉ — ÉTUDES PRÉLIMINAIRES)
(2ᵉ DEGRÉ — ÉTUDES GÉNÉRALES)
(3ᵉ DEGRÉ — ÉTUDES SPÉCIALES)

CERTIFICAT

Nous attestons que M ——————

demeurant à —————— *rue* —————— *nᵒ* ——

a subi avec ——————

l'examen d'études astrologiques du —————— *degré.*

Bruxelles, le ——————

LES MEMBRES DU JURY :

VICE-PRÉSIDENT   *PRÉSIDENT*   *PROFESSEUR*

♈ **ARIES.**

♉ **TAURUS.**

♊ **GEMINI.**

The twelve signs of the Zodiac and their symbols from 'The Astrologer of the Nineteenth Century' (London, 1825).

also published books to educate an eager public how best to use the benefits and avoid the pitfalls of their own particular sun signs.

Astrology During the War

It must be admitted that most of these latter-day English prophets somehow failed to foresee the outbreak of World War Two, but, there again, prominent politicians shared this short-sightedness and they could hardly claim that their eyes were firmly fixed on the stars. Once the war began the forecasts were cheering rather than correct: the war would end very soon, and Hitler would go mad or die!

In 1939 *Hitler's Last Year of Power* was published. The author, 'Leonardo Blake', assured his readers there would be no war. Hitler and Goebbels would fade away, and even Churchill would retire from active life. In the first year of war a sequel to this book appeared, entitled optimistically *The Last Year of the War and After*, which predicted that the war would be over in the middle of 1940. There were various prophesies which threatened Hitler with 'universal law', and Germany with dark days.

The inaccuracies of Blake and his kind did not seem to trouble their devoted public. Optimistic but fallacious predictions may have been astrological error or, later in the war, part propaganda. At first glance this belief in the 'stars' in times of stress may seem too trivial to be recorded,

but a number of people felt it serious enough to be investigated. In 1941 the *New Statesman and Nation* published an article by the anthropologist, Tom Harrisson, on 'Mass Astrology', which gave the findings of the social effects of popular astrology as provided by the English newspapers: the appeal was to a 'constant emphasis on the bright side'.

Our modern reaction might be that when established religion no longer comforts, people seek some alternative set of cosmic beliefs. Yet, such misplaced optimism during a world crisis could be dangerous, hiding the truth from people and giving them a fatalistic 'what will be will be' attitude – so good for an enemy's morale.

At a literary luncheon in November 1941 some of the stargazers justified their beliefs, and highlighted their successes. Certainly, R. H. Naylor had a better record than most other astrologers, for he seems to have forecast the German invasion of Norway, France's surrender, and Japan's and America's involvement in the war.

The potential risk to British security posed by popular astrology eventually gave rise to questions in the House of Commons in June 1942. A Conservative M.P. quoted a prediction by Edward Lyndoe in the newspaper *The People*, which suggested that Germany could never invade England, and demanded of the minister of information 'Whether his attention had been

♎ **LIBRA.**

♏ **SCORPIO.**

♐ **SAGITTARIUS.**

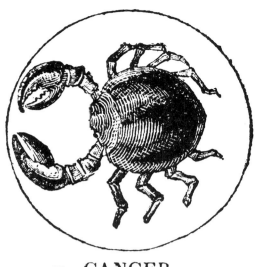

♋ CANCER.

♌ LEO.

♍ VIRGO.

drawn to the fact that astrologers are predicting that Germany is on the brink of collapse; and whether he will stop astrological predictions about the war in order to counteract the risk that addicts of astrology will relax their efforts?'

Brendan Bracken, the minister concerned, pointed out that astrologers in other papers thought Germany could invade England and answered: 'Astrologers seem to have the misfortune to be perpetually in conflict. And, as no sensible person takes their predictions seriously, I cannot ask our overworked censors to meddle in their mysteries.'

As it happened a government department took astrology seriously enough to employ Captain Louis de Wohl as its 'astrologer extraordinary'. A Hungarian by birth, who had lived in Germany and then adopted England as his homeland, de Wohl was an able author and journalist. He wrote a book on St Thomas Aquinas, which was favourably received, and it is difficult to ascertain just how much credence he placed in astrology. He had been a keen amateur astrologer and turned to it professionally only when he arrived in London. His social connections allowed him to make contact with those in influential positions. His prewar predictions had hardly been successful: he declared Neville Chamberlain's horoscope to be fortunate and that Gandhi would die in 1939. During the war he asserted that Hitler knew that

fortune was turning against him, and that the Allies were employing astrology. Also, according to de Wohl, Benito Mussolini's horoscope (cast in 1941) was excellent, although he would have 'a violent and sudden end'. De Wohl's autobiographical book, *The Stars of War and Peace*, makes fascinating reading, but it is difficult to know what is accurate and what is hindsight, astrological licence, or wishful thinking. However, by now we ought to be accustomed to the writings of astrologers. He explained how his first wartime task was to work out Hitler's horoscope in order to see what Hitler's own astrologers ought to be telling him. De Wohl's superiors could then make calculated guesses as to how much astrological advice reached Hitler, or how the astrologers might have tempered their readings in order not to fall foul of the Führer!

Undoubtedly both sides employed astrology for propaganda purposes in the war. British Intelligence even produced fake numbers of a German occult magazine *Zenit* to get their propaganda across. The predictions were actually written after the events they described but it was hoped the readers would never know and be suitably deterred. There is very little evidence to suggest that Hitler either believed in, or personally employed astrologers, although other Nazi leaders certainly leaned towards the occult, and much has been written in order to

♑ CAPRICORN.

♒ AQUARIUS.

♓ PISCES.

COSMIC CLOCK   by Warren Kenton ©

Above:
Cosmic Clock. A diagram designed by Warren Kenton as a fusion of astrological principles.

Right:
Zodiac 'personality' poster—an example of the present-day vogue of astrology. Reproduced by kind permission of Personality Posters.

demonstrate that Hitler shared their views.

However, before we examine the Nazi attitude to astrology, and what de Wohl appeared to be combating on behalf of the Allies, we ought to glance at how prewar Germany treated the subject. In times of national disillusion and despair people turn for consolation towards the occult, and this was particularly true in Germany after the First World War, where the interest in astrology and all things mystic blossomed more thickly than anywhere else in Europe. Although the Germans produced many books and publications dealing with the subject at serious and popular levels, eventually prohibited by the Nazis, the newspaper star column was not introduced until after the Second World War.

One of the best-known serious German astrologers was Elsbeth Ebertin. In 1923 someone sent her Hitler's date (although not hour) of birth, and in her *Prophetic Annual* she published a character reading which warned that this sort of individual would be associated with political disruptions which would prove unfortunate in late autumn. At the close of 1923 Hitler was associated with an attempted *Putsch* and imprisoned. One may wonder whether during this time he remembered his reaction to Elsbeth Ebertin's prophecy when he was alleged to have said: 'What have women and the stars got to do with me?'

The Weimar Republic had plenty of supposedly serious astrologers, whose theories smacked blatantly of racialism. When Hitler came to power in 1933 astrological magazines were supressed and several astrologers 'removed', even the German branch of the Theosophical Society being shut down. Astrology had not always shown itself in favour of the Nazi

Michel Gauquelin who has made an extensive study of the relation between cosmic and biological phenomena.

Opposite page:
Astrology has attracted artists of all kinds. Two scenes from the ballet 'Horoscope', first produced in 1938, which portrays a man and a woman born under two conflicting signs and brought together by the moon in their mutual sign Gemini.

party, and Hitler's horoscope had provided astrological headaches, since the astrologers had to try to 'doctor' the chart which suggested his career might well end in disaster. Although astrological conferences had been popular in Germany since 1922 the one held in 1938 was only permitted (with the Gestapo in attendance) provided none of its proceedings were published. From what we have already seen of the history of astrology the Nazi attitudes to it might be compared with that of certain Roman emperors who wished to proscribe astrology and eliminate astrologers lest they and their art foretell a less-than-perfect future for those in power.

Yet the preoccupation of Himmler and other Nazis with occult matters is well known. Despite the ban on such things a Dr Fesel, who had some connection with Himmler's department, asked the Swiss statistician, Karl Ernest Krafft, who was living in Germany and was an admirer of the regime, to make some economic predictions based on planetary positions. As a bonus – and a dangerous one at that – Krafft, who had been examining Hitler's horoscope, warned that he would be in danger during the early part of November 1939. The Munich bomb plot failed to kill Hitler. Krafft was arrested on suspicion of complicity, but managed to explain that the source of his information was cosmic rather than human. This resulted in him being drawn into the Nazi propaganda machine.

Krafft's story is an intriguing one. He did not consider himself as an astrologer but a statistician who was fascinated by astrology, and called himself a 'psychological consultant'. For almost ten years before his involvement with the Nazis he had examined the details of planetary positions at the time of birth of some 2000 musicians to try to discover some correspondence. Krafft also studied charts of members of the same family in an attempt to find out whether there were any similar planetary aspects linking the births of different generations. During this century there have been many such attempts at proving the validity of astrology in terms of statistics and the results have been tantalising rather than conclusive. However, until Krafft's experiments nobody had gone to such pains. Despite his obviously dedicated and careful research the 'regular' scientists at the University of Geneva were unimpressed, as were the German astrologers, although some of them were following similar ideas, and eventually Krafft concluded astrology to be 'irrational'. Only later did some scientists and psychologists, like Jung, pursue his theories.

Krafft's *Treatise in Astrobiology*, published in 1939, has impressed some serious postwar astrologers, although Michel Gauquelin, the French psychologist and statistician, who conducted similar although more elaborate experiments in the 1950s, wrote scathingly in his own *Astrology and Science* that Krafft had made enormous astronomical errors on nearly every page of the work, and he also found fault with Krafft's use of statistics.

Rather in the style of the medieval astrologers, Krafft turned to investigating the planetary

Julia Parker, a consultant astrologer, is President of The Faculty of Astrological Studies, a non-profit-making teaching and examining body founded in 1948.

symbols in an attempt to link certain basic human temperaments with particular planets: this he termed 'typocosmy'.

Krafft was opposed to giving character readings without some kind of personal interview and, like some of today's serious astrologers, he would not make outright predictions for individuals because of 'moral and psychological dangers'. Nor did he care for 'progressing' the birth chart to make a reading for a particular year based on imagined computations of how the planets would have moved. Such complicated calculations are easily open to error and moreover, the native may quite unconsciously bring about the events predicted.

Louis de Wohl had learned of Krafft in a very roundabout manner through the Romanian ambassador in London. The latter had written to Krafft, and received a reply, that had first gone through the hands of the wily Dr Fesel and the Nazi propaganda department, although against Krafft's wishes. This hinted that the Swiss was hand-in-glove with the Nazis and was giving their leader astrological advice. There is no evidence that Krafft ever met Hitler, and it is difficult to imagine anyone daring to tell the Führer that the stars had plans which differed from his.

At the time de Wohl believed himself to be working against Krafft and other Nazi-orientated astrologers, the Swiss statistician was actually under arrest. When Rudolf Hess fled to Scotland in 1941, all astrologers fell under suspicion of having influenced Hitler's deputy. This was

The sort of objects with astrological associations popular in the latter half of the twentieth-century. From Zodiac, the Astrological Emporium, London.

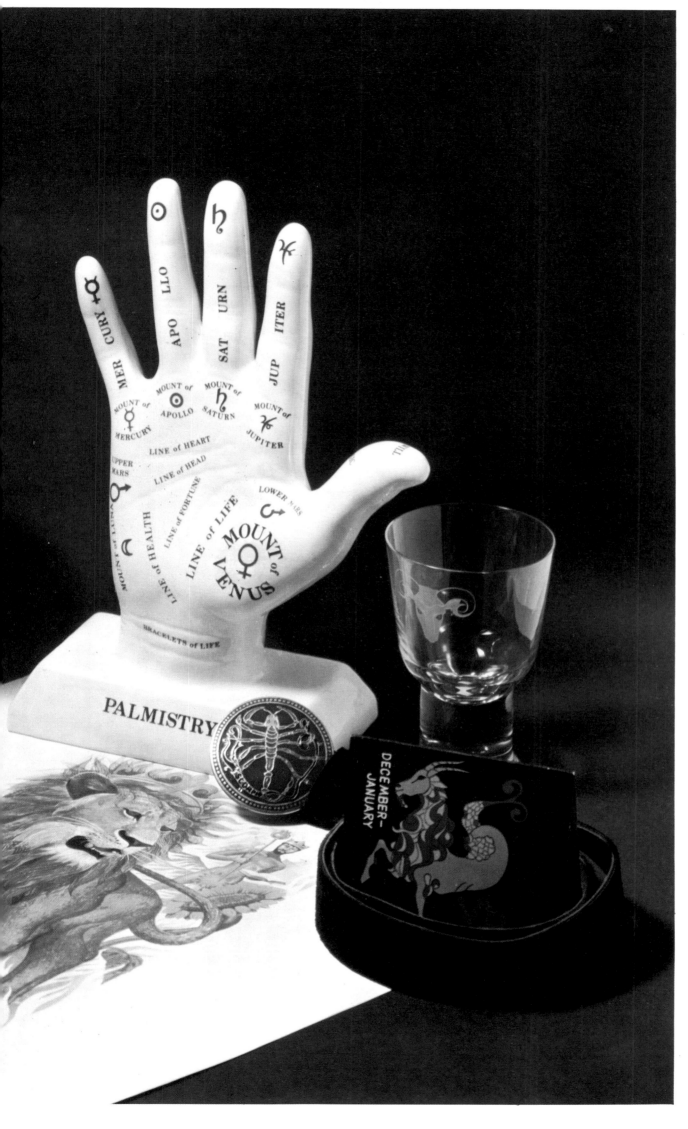

sufficient reason for the Nazis to decide that astrologers were working against their cause: and they were arrested and their books burnt. Totalitarianism, whether left or right, is naturally suspicious of anything as individualistic as astrology. After a while, many astrologers were released, but Krafft was not totally free. Instead he was coerced into working for the propaganda ministry. He refused to continue to allow his astrological work to be manipulated and died while on his way to a concentration camp.

Just how much astrology was used during World War Two and how successful it was would be hard to gauge. Joseph Goebbels who did not believe in astrology, but felt that 'crazy times call for crazy actions', wrote in his diary in 1942: 'In the United States astrologers are at work and predict an untimely end for the Führer. We are familiar enough with this type of propaganda for we have used it ourselves. Whenever we can, we will again exploit the possibilities which astrology has to offer. I anticipate important results from it, particularly in the U.S.A. and England . . . We will recruit on our side all the specialists in prophecy of every type. Nostradamus must once again authorize us to quote from him!'

From *The Last Days of Hitler* by Hugh Trevor Roper we learn that early in 1945, despite the official ban on astrology, Goebbels sent for the horoscopes of Hitler and Germany (carefully preserved in Himmler's research department). The horoscopes suggested that, though there would be disasters early that year, these would be followed by a great triumph in the second half of April and peace in August, and German greatness was assured for 1948.

On Friday 13th April Franklin D. Roosevelt

died, and Goebbels phoned Hitler: 'My Führer, I congratulate you. Roosevelt is dead. It is written in the stars that the second half of April will be the turning point for us!' He was right, but not the way he had envisaged.

The war over, German interest in astrology reflected the mood seen after World War One. With the return of prosperity astrology became a subject for popular magazines rather than serious study, but, nevertheless West Germany (and particularly Hamburg) has more serious scholars interested in astrology than elsewhere.

Astrology and Psychology

Before the outbreak of World War two, Dr Walter Koch had written several works on classical astrology as well as *Astrological Teachings Concerning Colours* and *The Soul of Gemstones*. Like other German astrologers he was imprisoned during the war and his books destroyed. Afterwards he and like-minded academics began examining the different arrangements of the twelve houses of the horoscope. Koch was also one of the founders of the Cosmobiological Society. One German group of cosmobiologists, led by Reinhold Ebertin, the son of Elsbeth Ebertin, believes that astrology can be improved only by eliminating much of the dead wood of traditional practices which date back to the *Tetrabiblos*, and are the fundamentals of many astrologers' craft. Such groups care little or nothing for the twelve house divisions or the signs of the zodiac, but take into account planetary aspects. The Hamburg School – to the consternation of traditionalists – also ignores the established zodiac. Instead it refers to eight 'hypothetical trans-Neptunian planets', and has even compiled ephemerides for them. Strangely enough the school seems to make excellent horoscope readings from its data!

Koch and others like him have been especially keen to find some link between astrology and psychology, which would detach the subject from 'fortune-telling' and put it on the more serious and acceptable plane of character analysis. Gradually, it has become realised that psychology and astrological symbolism are not too far apart. 'Determinism' is a modern word but means much the same as 'fate' as spoken of by the ancients. Present-day psychologists may examine background, environment, hereditary factors, and reactions. The astrologer-savants of long past would have done much the same thing when reading a horoscope.

The most famous psychologist to examine the question of astrology was C. G. Jung, who, in the 1950s, evolved the theory of 'synchronicity' – a description rather than an explanation which may account for its not having really become popular in scientific circles. Synchronicity ('an acausal connecting principle') is a method of trying to define an apparently significant relationship between particular events in the physical universe, which appear to have no evident causal link. Jung tried to demonstrate that certain happenings may appear to be related because they mean something similar to the observer, or may look as if the one caused the other, or may be purely coincidental.

A record sleeve for 'The Planets' by Gustav Holst. The theme of astrology continues to provide a source of inspiration for artists. Reproduced by kind permission of Decca Records.

Serious modern astrologers, relieved to be released from their less reputable fortune-telling associates, eagerly grasped at the idea of synchronicity, and used Jung's terminology to make their craft more plausible, and to give it respectability and an intellectual basis. Now, they might claim that the position of a certain planet – once held to cause particular events – merely coincided with those events.

While acknowledging man's use of and need for astrology to be compelling enough to require some non-causal reason, Jung could not believe there could be any causal connection between the life pattern of individuals on earth and stars billions of light years away.

According to Jung 'The primitive mentality has always explained synchronicity as magical causality right down to our own time, and on the other hand philosophy assumed a secret correspondence or meaningful connection between natural events until well into the eighteenth century. I prefer the latter hypothesis . . .'

As to the meaningfulness of the details of the birth chart Jung pointed out that 'Whatever happens in a given moment has inevitably the quality peculiar to that moment' and went on to show how experts in certain subjects could tell many things about an object from its appearance. 'And there are even astrologers who can tell you, without any previous knowledge of your nativity, what the position of the sun and moon was and what zodiacal sign rose above the horizon at the moment of your birth . . .'

Jung turned to astrology in an experiment to explore 'meaningful connections'. He took 966 horoscopes of married couples and tried to discover the variations in the charts of those married and non-married. The charts of the married pairs frequently demonstrated particular

A zodiac sundial on the wall of the Old Observatory at Greenwich. The lines on the dial represent the points of entry and exit of the sun into the various signs.

The Astrological Emporium, 3 Kensington Mall, London, W.8., specializes in astrology.

planetary aspects, viz: the Moon in conjunction with the Sun; the Moon in conjunction with the Moon; and the Moon in conjunction with the Ascendant . . . all traditional lunar aspects for marriage.

In *The Interpretation of Nature and the Psyche* Jung wrote: 'The fifty possible aspects to be considered in a marriage relationship were examined statistically. The result showed that in three quite fortuitously associated batches of marriage horoscopes the greatest frequency fell into three different lunar conjunctions. The probability of these three figures is far from being significant, because, if we take any number of marriage horoscopes, there is always a 1:1500 possibility of our getting a similar result . . .' He concluded: 'This meaningful arrangement is an exceedingly improbable one. It looks very like a conscious fraud, and its calculation was bedevilled by all manner of unconscious tendencies to twist the result in favour of astrology and synchronicity, despite there being a contrary tendency in the conscious mind of the person responsible . . .'

In these researches Jung did acknowledge the earlier work of his fellow Swiss, Krafft, although, like him, he was inclined to decide that statistics showed astrology to be an irrational phenomenon. 'If astrologers had concentrated more on statistics to justify scientifically the accuracy of their forecasts they would have found out long ago that their pronouncements rest on unstable predictions.'

Far from denigrating all astrologers Jung had

recognized that certain of them could make astonishingly correct predictions, but denied that stars played any part in prophesy. The astrologer had the powers of a medium or seer who had an intuitive glimpse into the future.

Jung's views on the collective unconscious and archetypes made him particularly interested in the richness of zodiacal symbolism, and also the cultural significance attached to those astrological eras brought about by the precession of equinoxes.

The world of cosmobiology is a bewildering one, but too fascinating to be omitted, so let us look at some of the pioneering work attempted on this new frontier. Between the wars the Russian professor Chizhevsky endeavoured to find a statistical relationship between the sun's eleven-year cycle and events on earth. Not all his findings proved scientifically acceptable, but his fundamental theory that the sun does affect life by producing ions (electrically charged particles formed by loss or gain by an atom of electrons) in the atmosphere has now been shown to be correct.

The German professor Bortels has since shown that changes in the weather, like chemical and microbiotic ones, seem to depend on solar radiation. The Italian scholar Piccardi elaborated on this theory to find that body and mind are continuously affected by influences from space, and this fact has now to be taken into account in calculations pertaining to physics.

The 'Takata effect' is the name of the result of researches of Professor Takata in Japan. Takata

discovered that man is a 'living sundial',
although the precise reasons behind this extraordinary fact are still under investigation.
Flocculation in the blood is affected not only by
the sun's cycle, but also by its rising and setting
and the eruptions on its surface.

Perhaps the most fascinating experiments on
the influences of sun and moon was carried out
by the American professor of biology, Frank
Brown. He took a selection of living organisms,
including a potato, a rat, oysters, and a fiddler
crab, and put them in a specially controlled
atmosphere, viz: temperature, pressure, light,
and humidity were kept at the same level,
which meant, in theory, that the subjects
could show no reaction whatsoever to the outside world.

Certainly the animals—and the potato—behaved in a biologically irregular manner. Brown
found that their 'internal clocks' could not be
functioning by themselves, but their rhythm

appeared to be set in motion by the solar or lunar
day or the relationship between the two. For instance, the rat, although enclosed in darkness,
was twice as lively when the moon set. Therefore, Brown concluded cosmic influences do
affect living organisms and, if this can happen in
an artificial atmosphere, how much more may it
be true under ordinary circumstances?

Gauquelin may have felt Krafft's approach
was mistaken, but nevertheless the Frenchman
carried out his own precise statistical survey of
the births of 25,000 Europeans of the professional classes. Unlike Krafft, who had to do much
of his research without this information, Gauquelin took infinite trouble to pin down the
exact hours of birth.

To his surprise, he discovered that a pre-
ponderance of births of men of particular
professions appeared to coincide with the rising
or zenith of particular planets as follows. Mars:
more scientists, doctors, athletes, soldiers, and

152

executives, but fewer writers, painters and musicians. Jupiter: more team athletes, soldiers, ministers, actors, journalists, and playwrights but fewer solo athletes, scientists, and doctors. Saturn: more scientists and doctors but fewer actors, painters, journalists, and writers. Moon: more ministers, politicians, and writers, but fewer athletes and soldiers.

These findings were greeted cautiously by other scientists. Astrologers' reactions were even less enthusiastic, possibly because they did not like the idea of their territory being encroached upon.

Gauquelin has also tried to trace the inherited resemblances in the horoscopes of children and their parents, but the results are highly debatable.

The ancients might be baffled at our manner of gathering statistical and scientific information,

but would probably greet many of the findings with an 'I told you so'. For some followers of astrology it would seem as if the whole business has come full circle once more.

The variety of theories supporting astrology in this century are as diverse as the arguments against it. While hosts of astrologers continue with traditional methods of charting and reading the horoscope, others sound positively heretical in their wish to shed classical teachings in favour of theosophical-style mysticism, liberally sprinkled with Jungian psychology (especially true in America), or employ quasi-scientific theories, or preach a highly complicated version of the microcosm and macrocosm. But all these go to show one thing: whatever its worth belief in astrology is not dead. William Lilly and those who came before might not recognize their present-day colleagues, but basically they are

A set of modern Israeli postage stamps, originally 20 by 40 millimetres in size, featuring the signs of the zodiac.

still pursuing the same idea.

All this takes us a long way away from the best-known aspect of twentieth-century astrology – the 'star columns'. If you are interested enough to conduct a simple experiment on your own account, get hold of as many magazines and newspapers as you can containing predictions for a similar period. Then compare what each has to say about your particular sun sign. If you can read other languages, or even other alphabets (you will find the 'stars' in Arabic and Greek, although these are quite likely to be syndicated and translated from some American or European publication) you will have an even wider selection. The devoted followers of such columns will always discover comforting similarities, while the non-believers will find their scepticism well-founded. Horoscopes, if they mean anything, are necessarily highly individual matters

as the next chapter will demonstrate, and astrology is too complex to be pinned down in a few trivial indeterminate phrases. It is to be hoped that this book has shown believers that there is a lot more to their faith than what the stars say about tomorrow, and perhaps the sceptics will no longer dismiss the subject as one unworthy of investigation.

Whatever the validity of astrology – and perhaps it will never be fully determined – the need for such a belief seems fundamental to mankind. During our long journey from Sumer to the present day, one fact emerges: man has always looked to the skies in an attempt to understand and define the meaning of existence and make provisions against the future. As we approach the Age of Aquarius, said by some astrologers to be the time of great spiritual awakening, there is no sign of this search ceasing.

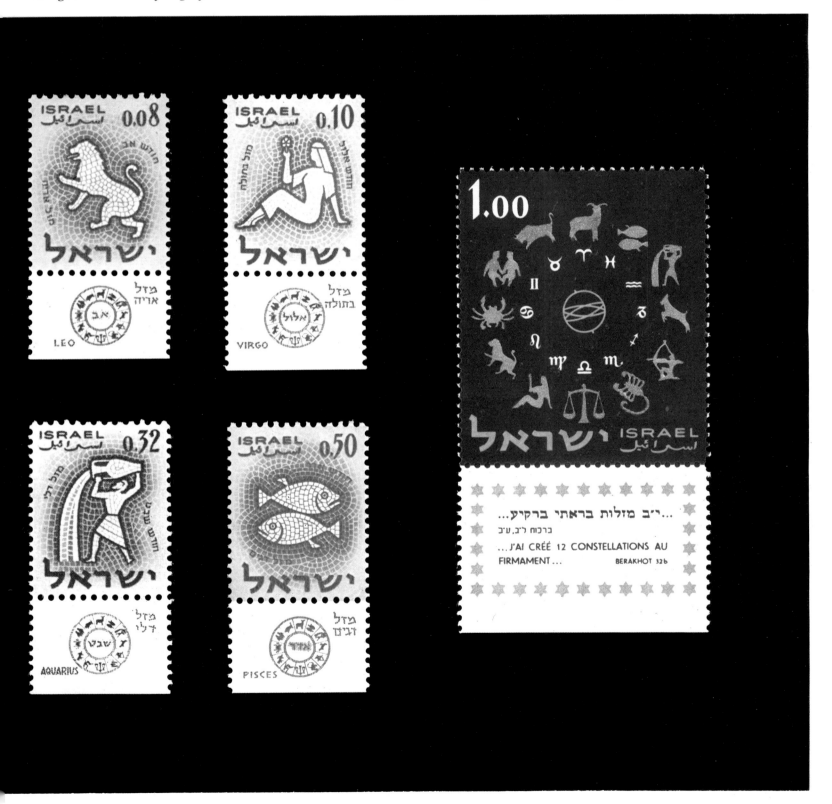

The Astrologer's Map

The wily advertiser is aware that you know your sun sign, as he knows his, and employs such 'personal' knowledge to sell products. If you are Aries (or any of the others) you may be tempted to buy (besides those invaluable glossy or humble publications that tell *you* about *your* character, fate, good and bad days and ideal mate) clothes, cosmetics, pottery, perfume, jewellery, and linen. And why shouldn't it be decorated with a zodiacal motif, especially for *you*, and therefore all those others who share that sign? If you are prepared to carry such a theory to its illogical conclusion then, according to this philosophy, there are only twelve types of people throughout the world.

Yet, if you have read this far you will understand that, whether or not you believe in astrology, it is much more complicated than that – its highly simplified, twentieth-century common denominator – and it would not be fair to leave you with this realization without explaining why.

This chapter aims to present a general picture of charting the horoscope as well as the meanings attributed to planets, houses, and zodiac. For those interested enough to pursue the subject at a more specialised level there are many excellent books available devoted entirely to the grammar of astrology and a selection of these is given at the back of the book.

Casting the horoscope

Anyone possessed of a knowledge of simple arithmetic may learn to chart a nativity by following the instructions in a text book. The horoscope is only a geocentric map of the position of the stars as if 'frozen' at the time of birth. To be able to interpret that map with any success is another matter, which requires some kind of intuitive skill as well as the ability to understand the meanings and aspects without continually referring to a text book.

Let us make a rough geographical comparison: you can probably make a decent copy of a relief map of South America, putting in the correct names and differentiating between high mountains and flat grasslands. Yet, only someone who has explored the lands and understood the people can really give you a vivid picture of what your map is all about. Otherwise it remains an outline on paper, and so it is with the horoscope devoid of a good astrologer's skill.

Stage *1* To hope to cast a horoscope with any degree of accuracy you need the date of birth, exact time of birth, place of birth, and its longitude and latitude.

Stage *2* Basic equipment: a protractor and a ruler, and a blank horoscope chart. How the twelve house divisions may vary will be discussed later. Alternatively, you can start from scratch if you enjoy simple geometry, and use compasses to inscribe your chart on a plain sheet of paper. In this case stick to the twelve equal house divisions as most astrologers do anyway. Borrow from the library, or buy from any comprehensive bookshop an ephemeris for the year in question. Raphael's (published by Foulsham) is the most readily available. This will show you

The planets, signs of the zodiac and the departments of life attributed to each house division. Sixteenth-century woodcut.

156

the exact position of everything in the solar system at a specified time. You will also need a table of houses – you may find this in the back of some ephemerides – since it indicates how to correct the calculations in terms of the native's birthplace. Perhaps, you are beginning to see why those 'mass' horoscopes cannot really be expected to be accurate.

Stage 3 In the ephemeris look up the sidereal time (s.t.) for midday on the day of birth in question. Sidereal time is a few minutes shorter than the twenty-four hours of the solar/clock day. The difference between the two times is 'the acceleration on interval'. Since the ephemeris cannot provide the equivalent s.t. for each moment of the day it gives it only for midday. Therefore if the actual birth took place before noon, *subtract* from the s.t. the difference between it and the birth time (plus ten seconds for every hour, which roughly equals the 'acceleration on interval'). If the birth took place after noon *add* the amount (plus, of course, the ten seconds per hour). Now you will have found the s.t. of birth.

Now comes one of the real problems in horoscopy. While most people know where they were born, not many know the precise moment of birth. Few are born exactly on the hour or half-hour. To make matters more complicated and to the delight of their opponents, astrologers are divided on what the moment of birth really means. Is it the baby's first cry? Or when the umbilical cord is severed? Or when the head emerges? Or the whole body? Or is fate determined at conception? Such questions have absorbed stargazers for centuries, and have also provided a useful 'escape clause' should a reading prove totally unsuitable. It also makes the sort of duplication of fate suggested by the phrase 'For all those born under Aries . . .' rather ridiculous, for a horoscope not only depends on the exact birth time of the native but also on the longitude of the birthplace. While twins naturally share the same birthplace the difference – be it only minutes – in birth times will ensure them quite separate horoscopes.

Stage 4 Longitude. Greenwich Mean Time (G.M.T.) is all very well for those with a Greenwich meridian, but for the rest local time must be turned into G.M.T. The degrees and minutes of longitude (east or west) must be multiplied by four to obtain minutes and seconds. For places east of Greenwich add this to the s.t.; for places to the west subtract. Now you have the s.t. for the time of birth and where it took place.

Stage 5 Exact latitude. Is the birth place north or south of the equator? Use the table of houses to find out at, whatever the calculated s.t. and the latitude of the birthplace, which degree of the zodiac was rising over the eastern horizon. This is the ascendant, and in any twenty-four hour period there are 360 possibles ones. Use the protractor to mark the ascendant on your blank chart. Then use a ruler to join this to the point exactly opposite: that is the descendant. The invaluable table of houses also provides the relevant mid-heaven (medium coeli or m.c.). Fill that in, and draw a line from it, bisecting the ascendant-descendant one, to the edge of the

circle: this is the imum coeli (i.c.). Now your chart is divided into four equal quadrants and angles.

Stage 6 The ascendant is the beginning or 'cusp' of the first house. To fill in the other eleven house boundaries consult the table of houses for the latitude concerned. Now you should have the twelve signs of the zodiac marked on the outer rim of your chart. Remember that their boundaries do not correspond to the inner perimeter of the next one. Now we encounter another hurdle. While most people would probably prefer to use the Placidus tables (named after the seventeenth-century Italian astrologer-astronomer Placidus de Tito) since they are easily available, there are other arrangements of tables, viz: Regiomontanus, Campanus, and the more recently invented *Gebürtsorthäuser* (produced by W. A. Koch). Unfortunately, these different methods, besides requiring a knowledge of trigonometry to chart them, do not produce the same results. While the ascendant and m.c. may well stay the same, the very uneven divisions will produce a quite different horoscope.

Stage 7 Now your chart is ready for the planets to be marked. You need the ephemeris to locate the planets. Saturn, Uranus, Neptune, Jupiter and Pluto are easily dealt with, since they move

Astrologers casting a horoscope for the child being delivered in the foreground. From Jacob Rueff's 'De conceptu et generatione hominis' (Frankfurt-am-Main, 1587). E. P. Goldschmidt and Co Ltd.

only slowly. Find where they were at noon on the day of birth and mark them on your chart. Annoyingly enough for those who dislike calculations, Venus, Mercury, the Sun and Moon are fast moving, and their positions will need some adjustment between noon and the actual time of birth. For births before noon consult the planet's motion for the day before, otherwise look up where it was on the day of birth. At the back of the ephemeris are the log tables. Look up the log for the motion of the planet: a simple matter of running your eye along the columns marked degrees or hours, and down the one marked minutes – where these two marry up is the log. In the same manner look up the log for the hour of birth. Add these two logs together, and translate the total back into degrees to add it to the noon position of the planet according to the ephemeris. Now you have its position at the time of birth. Do not forget to convert Greenwich s.t. into local s.t. Some planets in the tables are marked 'R'. This means retrograde (i.e. they appear to go backwards in the zodiac, owing to the earth's motion). In this case you must subtract the movement on interval from the planet's noon position.

With these slow moving planets major aspects cannot occur very often. In a five-year period Saturn travels only sixty degrees, Neptune ten degrees, Pluto eight degrees, and Uranus twenty degrees. In that time the Sun will have travelled 1800 degrees, and the Moon would have made its journey about sixty times. So Sun and Moon conjunctions will occur monthly, and the other fast moving planets also regularly make fresh aspects with each other and the slow moving ones, but something like a Saturn-Jupiter conjunction can happen only about every 20,000 years.

Obviously, this means that everyone – whatever their birth month in any particular year – will have four planets in similar positions in their horoscopes. Except for the Moon, which travels from one sign of the zodiac to another every two or three days, the aspects of other planets during a week do not alter very radically, even if one or several have moved into the next sign.

If you want to draw a horoscope for anyone who lives in the Southern Hemisphere there are two points to be observed. There is no table of houses for these latitudes, so the ascendant will be the sign of the zodiac *exactly opposite* to that given in the tables for the Northern Hemisphere; and you have to add twelve hours to the s.t. you worked out for the time of birth. This makes up for the difference of sidereal time in southern latitudes. Incidentally, when you have completed these calculations you have to take off twenty-four hours to bring the time within the twenty-four-hour boundary of a day.

Stage *8* Now your birth chart should be ready for interpretation, and here the real headache begins. Most astrologers base their readings on the traditional and therefore long-accepted meanings found in a literature which is vast and still growing. Most tomes are eclectic rather than original: fundamentals do not alter very much, although, as language changes, it appears to be updating them. Remember that the ancient meanings have to be stretched somewhat to accommodate the discoveries of the nineteenth and twentieth centuries. Many authors, while acknowledging the works of those who have written before them, are inclined to denigrate certain theories or their presentation, subtly suggesting to the reader that their own more modern interpretations must be that much better. This means that the convinced student of astrology must wade through all those 'astrological cookbooks' so that the meanings for each planet, sign, house and aspect are imprinted in his mind.

Yet, even if you do master this maze of meanings, there are still other problems to tackle. For instance, the interpretation of the aspects is not completely agreed upon by the

pundits. You must take into consideration the quadruplicities and triplicities: an abundance of planets of any particular type is said to give the individual an ill-balanced character. It also matters whether there are more planets to the east or west, or below the ascendant-descendant line. You have to remember the traditional zodiacal and planetary types. While the majority of people are 'mixed', some serious astrologers claim that many individuals may be categorized as 'pure' and can pick out their sun sign and ascendant without first asking details of the birth date.

Despite these complications and ambiguities it is astonishing to find a host of astrological 'do it yourself' manuals that blithely provide no more than the accepted interpretations with-out so much as a hint of the problems.

Antagonists can sneer at the grammar and its inaccuracies, and make out a very strong case against astrology. Yet there are some remarkable instances when interpretative and predictive readings of horoscopes have proved accurate, and it would be hard to dub all these purely co-incidental. It may well be that they are a blend of clever interpretation and a good astrologer's intuitive powers.

While it is not too difficult to draw a birth chart from which the native may recognize certain character truths among the plethora of statements, the task of reading the future is much more hazardous and open to inaccuracies. Yet this is the main reason why people consult astrologers. Good modern practitioners prefer

A seventeenth-century French engraving depicting the influence of the moon on women. The female cycle, and therefore all women's moods, have long been attributed to the visiting moon.

Diagram of a blank horoscope showing twelve equal house divisions.

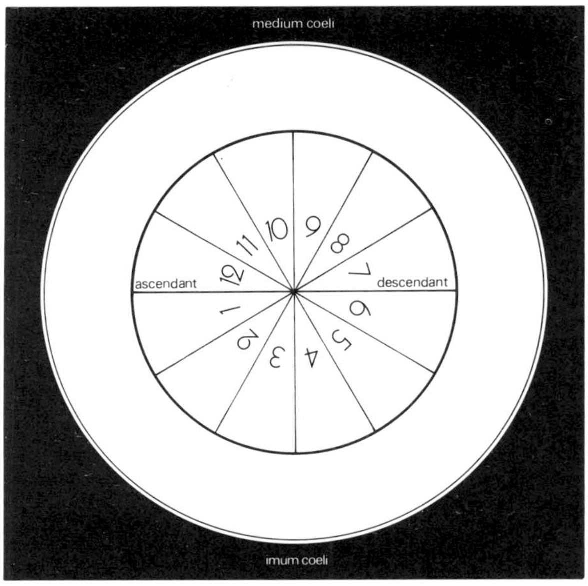

to avoid predictive charts, which are frequently drawn by progressing the horoscope by the 'day for a year' method. This simply means that if someone wants to know what will happen when he or she reaches the age of thirty the astrologer draws (using the ephemeris and table of houses naturally) and reads a horoscope for the thirtieth day after birth.

The Twelve Houses

Remember these remain in the same position, and are numbered one to twelve in an anti-clockwise direction, starting in the east so that the ascendant is always in the first house.

First House: The general character, appearance, and health of the native, and how he or she reacts to life. Raphael says: '. . . bears signification . . . of him who propounds a question, or

FULL MOON—June 12, 4*h*. 15*m*. *a.m.*

EPHEMERIS] **JUNE, 1976** 13

D M	Venus. Lat. ° ′	Venus. Dec. ° ′	Venus. Dec. ° ′	Mercury. Lat. ° ′	Mercury. Dec. ° ′	Mercury. Dec. ° ′	☽ Node. ° ′
1	0 S 24	21 N 1	21 N15	3 S 44	15 N23	15 N18	11 ♏ 11
3	0 19	21 29	21 43	3 54	15 14	15 13	11 5
5	0 15	21 55	22 7	4 0	15 14	15 17	10 59
7	0 10	22 19	22 30	4 1	15 22	15 28	10 52
9	0 S 5	22 40	22 49	3 59	15 37	15 47	10 46
11	0 0	22 58	23 6	3 52	15 59	16 13	10 39
13	0 N 4	23 14	23 21	3 43	16 28	16 44	10 33
15	0 9	23 27	23 32	3 30	17 2	17 20	10 27
17	0 14	23 37	23 41	3 15	17 40	18 0	10 20
19	0 18	23 45	23 47	2 58	18 21	18 43	10 14
21	0 23	23 49	23 51	2 38	19 5	19 27	10 8
23	0 28	23 51	23 51	2 17	19 50	20 12	10 1
25	0 32	23 50	23 49	1 55	20 35	20 57	9 55
27	0 36	23 47	23 N44	1 32	21 18	21 N39	9 49
29	0 41	23 40	—	1 7	21 59	—	9 42
30	0 N43	23 N36		0 S 55	22 N18		9 ♏ 39

Mutual Aspects.

1. ♂ ✱ ♇. 2. ☿ Stat.
3. ☉ ☍ ♆. ♀ ± ♅, △ ♇.
5. ☉ ∠ ♄. ♀ ✱ ♂.
6. ♀ ☍ ♆.
7. ☉ ⚺ ♃. ♂ △ ♆.
8. ♀ ∠ ♄. 9. ☉ ⚼ ♅.
10. ♀ ⚺ ♃. 11. ♀ ⚼ ♅.
12. ♅ P ♇.
13. ☉ P ♀. ☿ P ♃.
15. ☿ P ♂, ✱ ♄.
16. ☉ ⊥ ♃, ⊥ ♄. ♀ ⊥ ♃, ⊥
[♄. ♅ P ♇.
17. ☿ ∇ ♅. ♂ P ♃. ♃ Q ♄.
18. ☉ ☌ ♀. ♇ Stat.
19. ♂ □ ♃. 21. ☿ △ ♇.
22. ☿ Q ♂, ± ♅. ♀ ⚺ ♄. ♂
23. ☉ ⚺ ♄. ♀ △ ♅. [Q ♅.
24. ☉ △ ♅. ☿ P ♄, ☍ ♆.
25. ☿ P ♆. ♀ ∠ ♃.
26. ♂ ∠ ♇.
27. ☿ ∠ ♄. ♀ □ ♇.
28. ☉ ∠ ♃. ☿ ⚼ ♅. ♀ ∠ ♂.
30. ☉ □ ♇. ☿ ⚺ ♃. ♀ ∇ ♆.

D M	♆ Long. ° ′	♅ Long. ° ′	♄ Long. ° ′	♃ Long. ° ′	♂ Long. ° ′	♀ Long. ° ′	☿ Long. ° ′	Lunar Aspects. ☉	♇	♆	♅	♄	♃	♂	♀	☿
1	12 ♐ 39	3 ♏ 41	29 ♋ 37	15 ♉ 48	9 ♌ 5	6 ♊ 34	24 ♉ 58	∠					✱		∠	✱
2	12 ℞37	3 ℞39	29 43	16 2	9 39	7 48	24 D58		✱	⚼	□	☌		☌	✱	
3	12 35	3 37	29 49	16 15	10 14	9 1	25 2	✱	∠	△			□			
4	12 34	3 36	29 ♋ 56	16 29	10 49	10 15	25 10				✱	⚺				□
5	12 32	3 34	0 ♌ 2	16 42	11 23	11 29	25 24	□	⚺	□	∠	∠	△	⚺	□	
𝔖	12 30	3 32	0 8	16 56	11 58	12 42	25 41				⚺	✱	⚼	∠		△
7	12 29	3 31	0 14	17 9	12 33	13 56	26 3	△	☌	✱				✱	△	⚼
8	12 27	3 29	0 21	17 22	13 8	15 10	26 30	⚼		∠	☌	□			⚼	
9	12 26	3 27	0 27	17 36	13 43	16 23	27 0		⚺	⚺			☍	□		
10	12 24	3 26	0 34	17 49	14 17	17 37	27 35		∠		⚺	△				☍
11	12 22	3 24	0 40	18 2	14 52	18 51	28 15		✱	●	∠	⚼		△		
12	12 21	3 23	0 47	18 15	15 27	20 5	28 58	☍						⚼	☍	
𝔖	12 19	3 22	0 53	18 28	16 3	21 18	29 ♉ 45		□	⚺	✱		⚼			⚼
14	12 18	3 20	1 0	18 41	16 38	22 32	0 ♊ 36			∠			△			
15	12 16	3 19	1 7	18 54	17 13	23 46	1 31	⚼	△	✱	□	☍			⚼	△
16	12 15	3 18	1 13	19 7	17 48	24 59	2 29	△	⚼				□	☍	△	
17	12 13	3 16	1 20	19 19	18 23	26 13	3 32				△					□
18	12 11	3 15	1 27	19 32	18 59	27 27	4 38			□	⚼	⚼	✱			
19	12 10	3 14	1 34	19 45	19 34	28 40	5 47	□				△			□	
𝔖	12 8	3 13	1 41	19 57	20 9	29 ♊ 54	7 0		☍	△			∠	⚼		✱
21	12 7	3 12	1 48	20 10	20 45	1 ♋ 8	8 17			⚼			⚺	△		∠
22	12 5	3 11	1 55	20 22	21 20	2 22	9 37	✱			☍	□				
23	12 4	3 10	2 2	20 35	21			∠								
		3 9														

Extract from 'Raphael's Ephemeris for 1976' showing the longitudes of the planets and sidereal time for noon on each day of June 1976.

has his nativity cast; .. all questions are resolved by this house that relate to sickness, health, or long life; . . .'.

Second House: Possessions and money. Raphael says: 'In suits of law, or equity, it shows a man's friends or assistant; in private duels, it describes the querent's second; in eclipses, it shows the growing prosperity or adversity of a state or people . . .'.

Third House: Journeys, letters, telephone calls and all other kinds of communication. Close relatives and neighbours. Raphael says: 'The third house having signification of brethren, sisters, kindred and neighbours, and of all inland journeys, and of removing one's manufacture or business from one place to another . . .'.

Fourth House: Home matters. Place of birth. Parents. Underground places like caves and

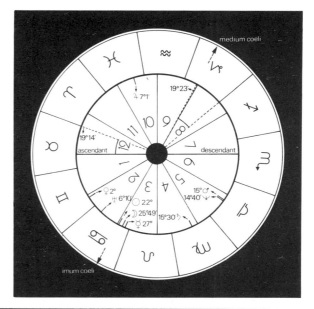

Diagram of a completed horoscope of a person born on July 15, 1950, in Manchester.

TABLES OF HOUSES FOR LONDON, Latitude 51° 32' N.

Sidereal Time.	10 ♈	11 ♉	12 ♊	Ascen ♋	2 ♌	3 ♍	Sidereal Time.	10 ♉	11 ♊	12 ♋	Ascen ♌	2 ♍	3 ♍	Sidereal Time.	10 ♊	11 ♋	12 ♌	Ascen ♍	2 ♍	3 ♎
H. M. S.	°	°	°	° '	°	°	H. M. S.	°	°	°	° '	°	°	H. M. S.	°	°	°	° '	°	°
0 0 0	0	9	22	26 36	12	3	1 51 37	0	9	17	16 28	4	28	3 51 15	0	8	11	7 21	28	25
0 3 40	1	10	23	27 17	13	3	1 55 27	1	10	18	17 8	5	29	3 55 25	1	9	12	8 5	29	26
0 7 20	2	11	24	27 56	14	4	1 59 17	2	11	19	17 48	6	♎	3 59 36	2	10	12	8 49	♎	27
0 11 0	3	12	25	28 42	15	5	2 3 8	3	12	19	18 28	7	1	4 3 48	3	10	13	9 33	1	28
0 14 41	4	13	25	29 17	15	6	2 6 59	4	13	20	19 9	8	2	4 8 0	4	11	14	10 17	2	29
0 18 21	5	14	26	29 55	16	7	2 10 51	5	14	21	19 49	9	2	4 12 13	5	12	15	11 2	2	♏
0 22 2	6	15	27	0♌34	17	8	2 14 44	6	15	22	20 29	9	3	4 16 26	6	13	16	11 46	3	1
0 25 42	7	16	28	1 14	18	8	2 18 37	7	16	22	21 10	10	4	4 20 40	7	14	17	12 30	4	2
0 29 23	8	17	29	1 55	18	9	2 22 31	8	17	23	21 51	11	5	4 24 55	8	15	17	13 15	5	3
0 33 4	9	18	♋	2 33	19	10	2 26 25	9	18	24	22 32	11	6	4 29 10	9	16	18	14 0	6	4
0 36 45	10	19	1	3 14	20	11	2 30 20	10	19	25	23 14	12	7	4 33 26	10	17	19	14 45	7	5
0 40 26	11	20	1	3 54	20	12	2 34 16	11	20	25	23 55	13	8	4 37 42	11	18	20	15 30	8	6
0 44 8	12	21	2	4 33	21	13	2 38 13	12	21	26	24 36	14	9	4 41 59	12	19	21	16 15	8	7
0 47 50	13	22	3	5 12	22	14	2 42 10	13	22	27	25 17	15	10	4 46 16	13	20	21	17 0	9	8
0 51 32	14	23	4	5 52	23	15	2 46 8	14	23	28	25 58	15	11	4 50 34	14	21	22	17 45	10	9
0 55 14	15	24	5	6 30	23	15	2 50 7	15	24	29	26 40	16	12	4 54 52	15	22	23	18 30	11	10
0 58 57	16	25	6	7 9	24	16	2 54 7	16	25	29	27 22	17	12	4 59 10	16	23	24	19 16	12	11
1 2 40	17	26	6	7 50	25	17	2 58 7	17	26	♌	28 4	18	13	5 3 29	17	24	25	20 3	13	12
1 6 23	18	27	7	8 30	26	18	3 2 8	18	27	1	28 46	18	14	5 7 49	18	25	26	20 49	14	13
1 10 7	19	28	8	9 9	26	19	3 6 9	19	27	2	29 28	19	15	5 12 9	19	25	27	21 35	14	14
1 13 51	20	29	9	9 48	27	19	3 10 12	20	28	3	0♍12	20	16	5 16 29	20	26	28	22 20	15	14
1 17 35	21	♊	10	10 28	28	20	3 14 15	21	29	3	0 54	21	17	5 20 49	21	27	28	23 6	16	15
1 21 20	22	1	10	11 8	28	21	3 18 19	22	♋	4	1 36	22	18	5 25 9	22	28	29	23 51	17	16
1 25 6	23	2	11	11 48	29	22	3 22 23	23	1	5	2 20	22	19	5 29 30	23	29	♍	24 37	18	17
1 28 52	24	3	12	12 28	♍	23	3 26 29	24	2	6	3 2	23	20	5 33 51	24	♌	1	25 23	19	18
1 32 38	25	4	13	13 8	1	24	3 30 35	25	3	7	3 45	24	21	5 38 12	25	1	2	26 9	20	19
1 36 25	26	5	14	13 48	1	25	3 34 41	26	4	7	4 28	25	22	5 42 34	26	2	3	26 55	21	20
1 40 12	27	6	14	14 28	2	25	3 38 49	27	5	8	5 11	26	23	5 46 55	27	3	4	27 41	21	21
1 44 0	28	7	15	15 8	3	26	3 42 57	28	6	9	5 54	27	24	5 51 17	28	4	4	28 27	22	22
1 47 48	29	8	16	15 48	4	27	3 47 6	29	7	10	6 38	27	25	5 55 38	29	5	5	29 13	23	23
1 51 37	30	9	17	16 28	4	28	3 51 37	30	8	11	7 21	28	25	6 0 0	30	6	6	0 0	24	24

Sidereal Time.	10 ♋	11 ♌	12 ♍	Ascen ♎	2 ♎	3 ♏	Sidereal Time.	10 ♌	11 ♍	12 ♎	Ascen ♎	2 ♏	3 ♐	Sidereal Time.	10 ♍	11 ♎	12 ♎	Ascen ♏	2 ♐	3 ♑
H. M. S.	°	°	°	° '	°	°	H. M. S.	°	°	°	° '	°	°	H. M. S.	°	°	°	° '	°	°
6 0 0	0	6	6	0 0	24	24	8 8 45	0	5	2	22 40	19	22	10 8 23	0	2	26	13 33	13	20
6 4 22	1	7	7	0 47	25	25	8 12 54	1	5	3	23 24	20	23	10 12 12	1	3	26	14 13	14	21
6 8 43	2	8	8	1 33	26	26	8 17 3	2	6	3	24 7	21	24	10 16 0	2	4	27	14 53	15	22
6 13 5	3	9	9	2 19	27	27	8 21 11	3	7	4	24 50	22	26	10 19 48	3	5	28	15 33	15	23
6 17 26	4	10	10	3 5	27	28	8 25 19	4	8	5	25 34	23	26	10 23 35	4	5	29	16 13	16	24
6 21 48	5	11	10	3 51	28	29	8 29 26	5	9	6	26 18	23	27	10 27 22	5	6	29	16 52	17	25
6 26 9	6	12	11	4 37	29	♐	8 33 31	6	10	7	27 1	24	28	10 31 8	6	7	♏	17 32	18	26
6 30 30	7	13	12	5 23	♏	1	8 37 37	7	11	8	27 44	25	29	10 34 54	7	8	1	18 12	19	27
6 34 51	8	14	13	6 9	1	2	8 41 41	8	12	8	28 26	26	♑	10 38 40	8	9	2	18 52	20	28
6 39 11	9	15	14	6 55	2	3	8 45 45	9	13	9	29 8	27	1	10 42 25	9	10	2	19 31	20	29
6 43 31	10	16	15	7 40	2	4	8 49 48	10	14	10	29 50	27	2	10 46 9	10	11	3	20 11	21	♒
6 47 51	11	16	16	8 26	3	4	8 53 51	11	15	11	0♏32	28	3	10 49 53	11	11	4	20 50	22	1
6 52 11	12	17	16	9 12	4	5	8 57 52	12	16	12	1 15	29	4	10 53 37	12	12	4	21 30	23	2
6 56 31	13	18	17	9 58	5	6	9 1 53	13	17	12	1 58	♐	4	10 57 20	13	13	5	22 9	24	3
7 0 50	14	19	18	10 43	6	7	9 5 53	14	18	13	2 39	1	5	11 1 4	14	14	6	22 49	24	4
7 5 8	15	20	19	11 28	7	8	9 9 53	15	18	14	3 21	1	6	11 4 46	15	15	7	23 28	25	5
7 9 26	16	21	20	12 14	8	9	9 13 52	16	19	15	4 3	2	7	11 8 28	16	16	7	24 8	26	6
7 13 44	17	22	21	12 59	8	10	9 17 50	17	20	16	4 44	3	8	11 12 10	17	17	8	24 47	27	8
7 18 1	18	23	22	13 45	9	11	9 21 47	18	21	16	5 25	4	9	11 15 34	18	18	10	26 6	29	10
7 22 18	19	24	23	14 30	10	12	9 25 44	19	22	17	6 7	4	10	11 19 34	19	18	10	26 6	29	10
7 26 34	20	25	24	15 15	11	13	9 29 40	20	23	18	6 48	5	11	11 23 15	20	19	10	26 45	♑	11
7 30 50	21			0	12	14			24	18	7 29	5	12	11 26 56	21	20	11	27		12
7 35					15															

Extract from 'Raphael's Emphemeris for 1976' showing part of a table of houses for London.

The beautiful city of Florence, birthplace of many great artists of the Renaissance, is ruled by Aries.

Opposite page:
A gold medal representing the sun. Gold is the metal associated with the sun.

The French author Honoré de Balzac (Sun in Taurus) wrote more than eighty novels. Statue by Auguste Rodin, Boulevard Raspail, Paris.

mines. Lands, houses and similar property. Raphael says: 'From the fourth house we resolve all questions in any way relating to or concerning the father of the querist. Also, all inquiries relating to land, houses, or estates, or to towns, cities, castles or entrenchments besieged, of treasures hidden in the ground, and all other questions relating to the earth, are answered out of this house, which is called the imum coeli, or angle of the earth.'

Fifth House: Enjoyment, love affairs, sensual pleasures outside marriage. Also paradoxically, children, education, all areas of entertainment and recreation. Raphael says: '. . . relative to children, and to women in the state of pregnancy; also all questions concerning the present health of absent sons or daughters, or the future health of those at home; inquiries relating to the real and personal effects of one's father, or concerning the success of messengers, ambassadors, or plenipotentiaries, or respecting the ammunition or internal strength of a place besieged . . .'. Is this a case of nineteenth-century puritanism rearing its head? Certainly there is no mention of either cerebral or fleshly pleasures.

Sixth House: Health, comfort, eating, general physical condition, servants/employees, pets, and weather as it affects wellbeing. Raphael says: '. . . servants or cattle. Also inquiries concerning the state of a sick person, whether curable or not, the nature of the disease, and whether of short or long duration; particulars relating to uncles and aunts, and all kindred on the father's side; also concerning one's tenants, stewards, or the like . . .'.

Seventh House: Marriage and business partners, all kinds of contracts and agreements, legal matters, and known enemies. Raphael says: '. . . love affairs and marriage, and to describe the person . . . that the querist will be joined with in marriage . . . all inquiries of the defendant in law-suits and litigations, or concerning our public enemies in time of war . . . it enables us

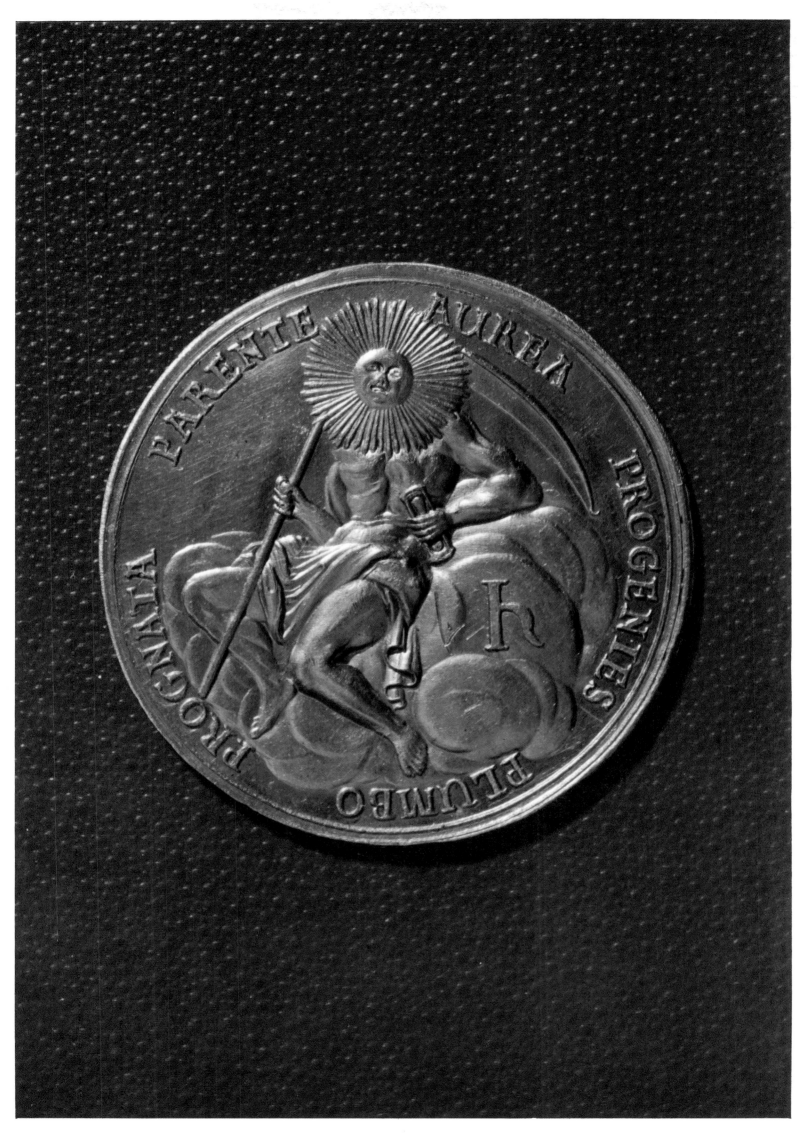

Queen Victoria is a Gemini type. Painting by G. Hayter.

if the wife be the querist . . .'.

Tenth House: Career, ambitions, possible honours and recognition. Also superiors, business and government. Raphael says: '. . . being the Medium Coeli, or most elevated part of the whole heavens, resolves all questions concerning kings, princes, dukes, earls, marquises, and all noblemen, judges, principal officers of state, commanders in chief, all orders of magistrates, and all persons in power and authority. Inquiries after preferment, honours, dignity, offices, places, pensions, or sinecures, or concerning the estate of kingdoms, empires, provinces, commonwealth, counties, cities, or societies of men . . .'.

Eleventh House: Friendships, advisers, dreams, financial position of those employed by native. Raphael says: '. . . friends and friendship, hope, trust, expectance, or desire; also whatever relates to the fidelity or perfidiousness of friends, or to the counsellors, advisers, associates, favourites, or servants of kings, princes, or men in power.'

Twelfth House: Misery, imprisonment, exile, hidden enemies, limitations. Raphael says: '. . . the house of tribulation . . . sorrow, affliction, trouble, anxiety of mind, distress, imprisonment, persecution, malice, secret enemies, suicide, treason, conspiracy, assassination, and everything appertaining to the misfortunes and afflictions of mankind.'

The houses have their own related signs and planets, although obviously they do not always marry up. First: Aries, Mars; second: Taurus, Venus; third: Gemini, Mercury; fourth: Cancer, Moon; fifth: Leo, Sun; sixth: Virgo, Mercury; seventh: Libra, Venus; eighth: Scorpio, Mars; ninth: Sagittarius, Jupiter; tenth: Capricorn, Saturn; eleventh: Aquarius, Saturn (Uranus); twelfth: Pisces, Jupiter (Neptune).

The Signs of the Zodiac

Remember that these are on the rim of your zodiacal chart, and move, unlike the fixed houses.

Aries

The Ram – 21st March to 20th April. Ruled by Mars. Cardinal. Fire sign. Equinoctial. Male. Eastern. Governs the head and brain. In the plant world rules lichens and seaweed type plants that prepare the ground for other kinds of vegetation. Those born under Aries are alleged to suffer with nervous disorders, headaches, depression, dyspepsia, and are thought to be deficient in phosphate of potassium. Because of this they are advised to eat tomatoes, dandelion leaves, lemons, celery, grapefruit, parsnips, and apples. Herbs to benefit their health include broom and wild cherry. An adventurous, enthusiastic and pioneering sign, inclined to impulsiveness, irritability and immature behaviour. Passion, conquests; an extremist politically.

Mars is obviously content in this sign, and the Sun exalts in it, but poor Venus is ill at ease. William Lilly also terms Aries as 'bestial, luxurious, intemperate, and violent . . .' and apportions to it such diseases as 'all gumboils,

to describe the person of the robber, by his shape, stature, complexion, and condition of life . . .'.

Eighth House: This is the house of death and loss, also matrimonial possessions, partner's property, wills and the like. Raphael says: '. . . concerning death, its time, quality, and nature, with all matters relating to legacies, wills, and last testaments; or who shall inherit the fortune and estates of the deceased. Inquiries on the dowry or portion of maids or widows; in duels, concerning the adversary's second; in law-suits, relative to the defendant's success and friends; and questions on public or private enemies, or concerning the substance and security of those we connect ourselves with in business . . .'.

Ninth House: Travelling, philosophy, religion, studies. Church affairs. Ideas. Raphael says: '. . . on the safety and success of voyages and travels into foreign countries; also inquiries of the clergy concerning church preferments, benefices, advowsons, and the like; and all questions relative to kindred and relations on the wife's side, and the same on the husband's side,

Dublin, seen here at night from the River Liffey, is under the sign of Taurus.

Page 166:
Mercury. The planet which reflects the changeable aspects of man's character is shown with his two houses Gemini and Virgo, presiding over a calm country scene. Miniature from 'De Sphaera', a fifteenth-century Italian manuscript. Biblioteca Estense, Modena.

Page 167:
Venus. The planet is naturally young, alluring and female, and presides over her two houses, Libra and Taurus. Beneath her is a scene of courtly love, very much the sort of picture associated with the storytellers in Boccaccio's 'Decameron'. Miniature from De Sphaera' a fifteenth-century Italian manuscript. Biblioteca Estense, Modena.

London is under the sign of Gemini. Seventeenth-century engraving.

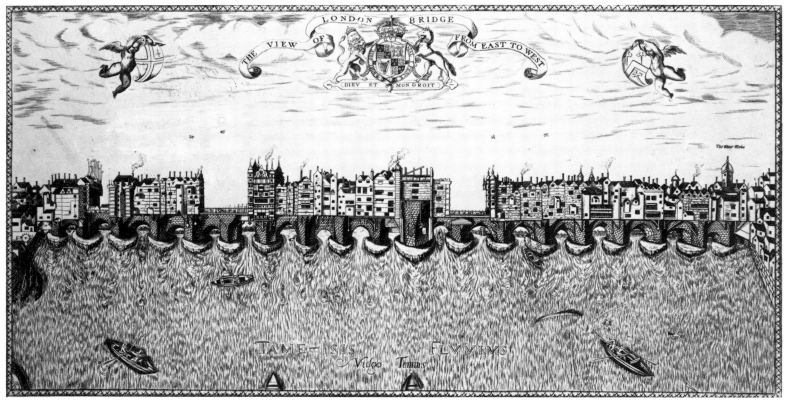

Mercurio di ragion lucida stella
Produce eloquenza gran fontana
Subtili ingiegni et ciaschunarte bella
Et e nimico dogni cosa uana :-

· VENVS ·

La gratiofa uener dil fuo ardore
Accende i cuo: gentili onde in cantare
Et danze et uaghe feste per amore
Induce col fuaue naghegoiare

The Dutch painter Rembrandt–
a self-portrait–is an example of
an artistic Cancer type.

the modern French writer on astrology, seems to agree with Lilly that Aries folk resemble rams. According to Lilly they have: 'A dry body, not exceeding in height; lean or spare, but lusty bones, and his limbs strong; the visage long, black-eye-brows, a long scraggy neck, thick shoulders; the complexion dusky, brown or swarthy.'

The Australian astrologer, Furze Morrish – one of the new-wave doyens – regards astrology as the supreme yogi who will change world thought and bring the self to enlightenment now that science and religion have been discredited. He sees the zodiac as a 'wheel of life and death', and Aries, as the initial sign, is ignorance whereas the ultimate sign, Pisces, represents universality. Famous people born with the Sun in Aries or Aries as their ascendant are Leonardo da Vinci, Vincent Van Gogh, Henry James, Marlon Brando, and Joseph Haydn.

Taurus

The Bull – 21st April to 21st May. Ruled by Venus. Fixed. Earth sign. Nocturnal. Female. Southern. Governs neck and throat. In the plant world rules fungi. Those born under Taurus are alleged to suffer with disorders of liver and kidneys, asthma and rheumatism, and are said to be in need of calcium, and sodium. Because of this they are advised to eat celery, apples, Swiss chard, spinach, radishes and strawberries. Beneficial herbs include burdock, coltsfoot, and yarrow.

A stable, balanced, and confident sign. Good family person. Stubborn, realistic, faithful, with occasional violent outbursts. Peace-loving and loyal to own class. Venus and Moon are content in this sign. William Lilly terms Taurus 'cold, dry and melancholy' whereas Raphael calls it 'bestial and furious'. To it Lilly apportions such diseases as sore throats, wens, throat ailments, and abscesses. Barbault sees a Taurus person as slow-walking and inclined to heaviness. William Lilly describes one as: '. . . a short, but full, strong and well-set stature; a broad forehead; great eyes, large swarthy face, and broad strong

swellings, pimples in the face, smallpox, hair lips [his own spelling!], polypus, ringworms, falling sickness, apoplexies, megrims, toothache, head-ache, and baldness.' Countries under the rule of Aries include England, Germany, Denmark, and Syria, and towns include Florence, Verona and Marseilles. André Barbault,

Venice is ruled by Cancer.
Seventeenth-century
engraving.

shoulders; great mouth, and thick lips; gross hands; black, rugged hair.' Very bull-like, and it is paradoxical that this sign is ruled by the planet associated with love and femininity. Countries and regions under Taurus are Ireland, Persia, Asia Minor, the southern parts of Russia, and the islands of Cyprus and Samos. Towns include Dublin, Parma and Leipzig. Famous people born with the Sun in Taurus or Taurus as their ascendant include Honoré de Balzac, Oliver Cromwell, Yehudi Menuhin, Bertrand Russell, and Johannes Brahms.

Gemini

The Twins – 22nd May to 21st June. Ruled by Mercury. Mutable or common. Air sign. Diurnal. Masculine. Western. Governs shoulders, upper arms and lungs. In the plant world rules mosses. Those born under Gemini are said to be prone to catarrh, bronchitis, eczema, and thought to be in need of potassium chloride. Because of this they are advised to eat the foods suitable for Aries, plus goat's milk, green beans, sprouts, watercress, and pineapple. Herbs to benefit their health include liquorice, tansy, vervain, and marigold.

Gemini is a lively, skilful, and versatile sign. Frequently unreliable, complex, and anxious. Likes to flirt, and is more interested in political theory than activity. Gemini people can be intellectual, egocentric, mad, but certainly fickle. Lilly sees Gemini producing all diseases and accidents associated with arms, shoulders or hands, as well as nervous illnesses. He describes Gemini people as '. . . upright, tall, straight . . . the complexion sanguine, not clear, but obscure and dark; long arms, yet many times the hands and feet short. and very fleshy; a dark hair, almost black; a strong. active body, a good piercing hazel eye, and wanton, and of perfect and quick sight; of excellent understanding, and judicious in worldly affairs.' Countries under Gemini include the United States and Belgium, and towns ruled by it are London, Versailles, Cordoba, New York, and Nuremberg. Famous people born with the Sun in Gemini or Gemini as their ascendant include Queen Victoria, Igor Stravinsky, Marilyn Monroe, and Harriet Beecher Stowe.

Cancer

The Crab – 22nd June to 22nd July. Ruled by the Moon. Cardinal. Water sign. Nocturnal. Female. Northern. Governs chest, elbows, breasts, and stomach. In the plant world rules horsetails, ferns, and club mosses. Those born under this sign are said to suffer with varicose veins, piles, and impaired vision, and are thought to be in need of calcium. Because of this they are recommended to eat red and green cabbages, watercress, kale, milk, prunes, onions, cottage cheese, egg yolks, parsley, and ryebread. Herbs which benefit their health include plantain, honeysuckle, and wintergreen.

An emotional and sensitive sign. Easily swayed. A real home- and family-lover. Inclined to be over-imaginative and shy. Strongly governed by childhood memories. Modern astrologers see the Cancer type as effeminate, which makes it easier for the females of this sign. Lilly describes this type as 'generally of low and small

Rome, the eternal city, is ruled by Leo. View from the Victor Emmanuel II monument.

stature, the upper parts larger than the lower; a round visage; sickly, pale, and white complexion; the hair a sad brown; little eyes; prone to have many children, if a woman.' A rather depressing picture! At least, John Varley, writing in his *Treatise of Zodiacal Physiognomy*, may see Cancer people as resembling crabs but allows them to have the crab's energy and tenacity. Lilly cites the diseases of Cancer as 'imperfections all over, or in the breast, stomach and paps; weak digestion, cold stomachs, rotten coughs, cancers, which are mostly in the breast . . .'. Zadkiel assures us that the disease, cancer, took its name from the zodiacal sign, since people born with it rising always have some illness in the breast!

Countries and continents ruled by cancer are The Netherlands, Scotland, and Africa. Towns include Constantinople, Algiers, Amsterdam, Cadiz, Venice, Genoa, New York, and Milan. Famous people born with the Sun in Cancer or Cancer as their ascendant include Henry VIII, Jean Cocteau, Rembrandt, Marc Chagall, and Ernest Hemingway.

Leo

The Lion – 23rd July to 23rd August. Ruled by the Sun. Fixed. Fire sign. Diurnal. Masculine. Eastern. Governs upper back, forearms, wrists, spine, and heart. In the plant world rules those bearing cones. People born under this sign are advised to keep their blood in good condition, and

Page 170:
The Sun, traditionally regarded as a planet by ancient astrologers. The elderly kinglike figure presides over his single house Leo. In the horoscope the Sun reveals the basic nature which will determine the individual's future. The scene shows young men practising talents which may help them later on in life. Miniature from 'De Sphaera', a fifteenth-century Italian manuscript. Biblioteca Estense, Modena.

Page 171:
Mars, the god of war, is shown with his two houses, Scorpio and Aries, presiding over a battle scene. Miniature from 'De Sphaera', a fifteenth-century Italian manuscript. Biblioteca Estense, Modena.

·SOL·

Il sole adbono: lubomo et gloria sprona
   Et doglii leggiadoria si dilecta
   Si sapienza porta la corona
Et di religion produce secta

· MARS ·

Il bellicoso marte sempre infiama
Li animi alteri al guerreggiare et sforza
Hor questolor quello ne satia sua brama
In lacquistar: ma piu sempre rinforza :

to the top in politics. Commanding, ambitious, and proud; sometimes selfish. An extrovert with a good intellect. The adverse side can produce arrogance and suspicion. Lilly gives the king of the beasts some nobility: 'a great round head; large prominent eyes, as if staring out, or goggle eyes, quick sighted; a full and large body, and more than of middle stature; broad shoulders, narrow sides, yellow or dark flaxen hair, and it curling or turning up; a fierce countenance, but ruddy high sanguine complexion; strong, valiant, and active; step firm and mind courteous. He notes the Lion's diseases as 'all sicknesses in the ribs and sides, as pleurisies, convulsions, pains in the back, trembling or passion of the heart, violent burning fevers; all weakness or diseases in the heart, sore eyes, the plague, the pestilence, the yellow jaundice.' Leo rules France and Italy, and the towns of Rome, Prague, and Philadelphia, and also the Alps and ancient Chaldea. Famous people born with the Sun in Leo or Leo as their ascendant include C. G. Jung, George Bernard Shaw, Napoleon, T. E. Lawrence, and Aldous Huxley.

Comparison of the attributes of Cancer and Leo demonstrates most vividly how the signs of the zodiac seem to alternate in their characteristics.

Virgo

The Virgin – 24th August to 23rd September. Ruled by Mercury. Mutable. Earth sign. Nocturnal. Feminine. Southern. Governs abdomen, hands, and intestines. In the plant world rules sedges, cereals, and grasses. Those born under this sign are said to suffer from pneumonia, colds, coughs, catarrh, pleurisy, and need plenty of potassium sulphate. They are recommended the foods suitable for Aries, with, in addition, the herbs rosemary, valerian, and motherwort.

Once this sign was thought of as a young maiden, but later she became an older woman with rather pedantic views. Intelligent, precise, clean, and observant. A practical supporter of

are said to need plenty of magnesium phosphate, to be found in plums, peas, wheat bran, oats, cocoa, oranges, lemons, and lettuces. Beneficial herbs are sorrel, dill, fennel, and mint.

A dominant, positive, strong-willed, idealistic, and independent sign. Leadership – whether establishment or revolutionary. Liable to rise

View of the old town of Jerusalem. The holy city for three religions, it is under the sign of Virgo.

order. Usually critically inclined and patient, with none of the flamboyance of the last sign. Lilly sees the Virgo type as having 'A slender body, rather tall, but well composed; a ruddy, brown complexion; black hair, well favoured or lovely, but not a beautiful creature; a small, shrill voice, all members inclining to brevity; a witty, discreet soul, judicious, and exceedingly well spoken; studious, and given to history, whether man or woman.' He cites Virgo's diseases as those of belly, bowels and testicles, and makes it the donor of worms, and cholic. Countries and regions under Virgo are Turkey, Switzerland, and the West Indies. Towns include Paris, Toulouse, Jerusalem, and Babylon. Famous people born with the Sun in Virgo or Virgo as their ascendant include Savonarola, Queen Elizabeth I, Cardinal Richelieu, and Greta Garbo.

Libra

The Scales – 24th September to 23rd October. Ruled by Venus. Cardinal. Air signs. Diurnal. Masculine. Western. Libra governs the lower back and kidneys. In the plant world rules iris, lilies, and orchids. Librans are alleged to need to maintain a balance between the acids and normal fluids of the body, and require sodium phosphate. They are advised to eat the same food as Taureans, and specially beneficial herbs are meadowsweet, celery tops, and dandelion.

Libra being an equinoctial sign and exactly opposite Aries is equally opposite in characteristics. It shares many of the Taurean qualities of gentleness and love, although it is the only non-bestial and non-human sign of the zodiac. Librans are naturally balanced and diplomatic. They have moderate politics and show understanding to their loved ones. They are also sociable, harmonious, and peace-making.

Lilly is highly complimentary about the Libra individual 'a well-framed body . . . beautiful visage . . . eyes generally blue . . . temper even . . .', although he cites the sign's diseases as gravel in the kidneys or bladder, and weakness in the back. China, Japan, and the parts of India nearer Persia are all governed by Libra, as are the towns of Lisbon, Vienna, Antwerp, and Frankfurt. Famous people born with the Sun in Libra or Libra as their ascendant include Lord Nelson, Franz Liszt, Graham Greene, T. S. Eliot, and Brigitte Bardot.

Scorpio

The Scorpion – 24th October to 22nd November. Ruled by Mars. Fixed. Water sign. Nocturnal. Feminine. Northern. Governs the pelvis and reproductive system. A sinister sign: perhaps because it is the eighth, as is the House of Death, and to increase its forbidding reputation many astrologers put Scorpio under the rule of the recently discovered Pluto. In the plant kingdom Scorpio rules all plants with phallic connections, viz: palms and aroids. Those under this sign are alleged to suffer with boils, ulcers, carbuncles, abscesses, and liver and kidney troubles, and are said to need calcium sulphate, which means they are recommended to eat the foods for Cancer, plus the herbs sarsparilla, marigold, wormwood, and horseradish.

Lilly describes this sign as normally repre-

Mosque at Marrakesh, Morocco. This country is said to be ruled by Scorpio.

Page 174:
February. Page from 'Les très riches heures du Duc de Berry' illustrating the zodiacal year. Fifteenth-century French manuscript. Musée Condé, Chantilly.

Page 175:
January. Page from 'Les très riches heures du Duc de Berry'. Fifteenth-century French manuscript. Musée Condé, Chantilly.

senting 'subtle, deceitful men', with 'a corpulent, strong able body, somewhat a broad or square face; a dusky, muddy complexion, and sad dark hair, much and crisping; a hairy body somewhat bow-legged-, short-necked; a squat, well-trussed fellow.' which is inclined to make the reader wonder at the appearance of the female counterpart! However, do not worry if you are a Scorpio: you are probably both aggressive and sexy. This sign is instinctive, passionate, rebellious, and also morbid. A political extremist. Lilly cites its diseases as 'Gravel . . . in the secret parts or bladder, ruptures, fistulas, or the piles; priapisms, all afflictions of the private parts . . . ' Morocco and Norway are ruled by Scorpio, as are the the towns of Ghent and Liverpool. Famous people born with the Sun in Scorpio or Scorpio as their ascendant include Martin Luther, Pablo Picasso, Fyodor Dostoevski, Marie Curie, and Jawaharlal Nehru.

Sagittarius

The Archer – 23rd November to 21st December. Ruled by Jupiter. Cardinal. Fire sign. Diurnal. Masculine. Eastern. In the plant kingdom rules great trees like oak, beech, and elm. Sagittarius governs hips and thighs, and the sacral area. Those born under it may suffer from a deficiency of silica which produces poor skin, nails, and hair, and consequently are advised to eat parsnips, asparagus, cucumbers, black figs, rye, and cherries. Beneficial herbs include chicory, burdock, dandelion, hawthorn, and red clover.

174

Greta Garbo (Sun in Virgo) has remained a famous name in the cinema, although she has not appeared in a film for many years.

This is the sign of the good-natured leader: a hunter rather than a leader, but with a considerable ability to get things done. Usually on the side of the oppressed. Honest and straightforward in love unless crossed, in which case promiscuous. Intelligent, loyal, but if the need arises rebellious. Morrish sees this fiery sign as 'the blue fire at the heart of the flame. This is the hottest part of the flame'. Lilly sees those born under 'Sagittary' as possessing 'a well-favoured countenance, somewhat long visage, but full and ruddy, or almost like sunburnt, the hair light chestnut colour, the stature somewhat above the middle size, a conformity in the members, and a strong, able body; inclined to baldness, and one fond of horses.' Certainly, as far as tradition is concerned, the Sagittarian is fond of riding and all sports. Not surprisingly Lilly cites the diseases of the Sagittarian as 'falls from horses, or hurts from them or four-footed beasts; also prejudice by fire, heat, and intemperateness in sports.' Countries and regions ruled by this sign include Yugoslavia, Hungary, Arabia, and Spain, and towns are Cologne, Avignon, Narbonne, and Toledo. Famous people born with the Sun in Sagittarius or Sagittarius as their ascendant include Winston Churchill, John Milton, James Thurber, and Mary, Queen of Scots.

Capricorn

The Goat—22nd December to 20th January. Ruled by Saturn. Cardinal. Earth sign. Nocturnal. Feminine. Southern. Capricorn governs knees and bones. In the plant kingdom it rules flowers with separate petals. Those born under this sign are said to have a tendency to a deficiency in calcium phosphate which can cause Bright's Disease, rickets, anaemia, catarrh, boils, deafness, and rheumatism, and they are recommended to follow the same diet as Cancer and Scorpio. The most beneficial herbs for them are plantain, black hellebore, elder, knapweed, and cinchona.

This is a reserved, uncommunicative, and self-disciplined sign. Diplomatic and traditional. Does not get on very well with the overbearing exuberance of Leo, and is advised to avoid alcohol. Remember that this sign was evolved from a 'goat fish' so Varley allows Capricorn folk to be either like a goat or a fish! Despite calmness and wit Capricorn people may be subject to pessimism and melancholy. Lilly sees them as 'not high of stature, long, lean, and slender visage; thin beard, and black hair, a narrow chin, long small neck, and narrow chest. I have found many times Capricorn ascending, the party to have white hair, but in the seventh very black.' He cites its diseases as fractures or strains of the knees, and, more alarmingly, leprosy and other skin ailments. Countries under Capricorn include India, Greece, Albania, Bulgaria, Mexico, and towns and regions include Oxford, and the Orkney Islands. Famous people born with the Sun in Capricorn or Capricorn as their ascendant include Joan of Ark, Woodrow Wilson, Pablo Casals, and Albert Schweitzer.

Aquarius

The Water-carrier—21st January to 19th February. Traditionally ruled by Saturn although some astrologers give Uranus as its joint ruler.

Winston Churchill was one of the most famous world leaders to be born under Sagittarius.

176

Fixed. Air sign. Diurnal. Masculine. Western. Governs lower legs and ankles. In the plant kingdom rules flowers with united petals. Those born under this sign are said to suffer from dropsy, catarrh, diarrhoea, goitre, and delirium tremens, unless they take in enough ordinary salt. Table salt will not do, since an excess leads to skin complaints, and so Aquarians are advised to follow the diet of Taureans; specially beneficial herbs include balm, valerian, tansy, and ladies' slipper.

This is an ethereal, idealistic and emotional sign. Those born under it are inclined to devote themselves to causes, and are loving, progressive, fond of innovation and reforms. Uranus may lend certain Aquarians a scientific bent as well as a longing for 'the brotherhood of man'. Morrish regards this sign as 'the awakener' who will develop spiritual awareness through meditation. It is not, therefore, surprising that believers in such abstractions look forward to the Age of Aquarius, although some astrologers insist this has already begun. Lilly does not describe Aquarians as precisely airy, rather of 'a squat, thick corporature . . . long visage, sanguine complexion . . . ' Other experts say Aquarian men possess beautiful feminine faces. According to Lilly Aquarian diseases affect legs and ankles, and include spasmodic and nervous complaints, cramps, and wind. Being a totally human sign it has all the inherent faults and virtues. Countries under Aquarius include Afghanistan and Russia, and towns are Hamburg, Bremen, and Piedmont. Eclipses occurring in this sign are said to cause great changes in England and comets herald that country's involvement in war. Famous people born with the Sun in Aquarius or Aquarius as their ascendant include Mozart, F. D. Roosevelt, James Dean, Francis Bacon, Charles Darwin, and Galileo.

Pisces

The Fishes – 20th February to 20th March. Ruled by Jupiter although some astrologers claim the watery Neptune to be its ruler instead. Mutable. Water sign. Feminine. Northern. It governs the feet, liver, and lymphatics. In the plant world it rules, not surprisingly, seaweeds and algae. Those born under this sign are alleged to suffer from a deficiency in iron which can result in low blood pressure, anaemia, haemorrhages, heavy periods, and inflammation. They are advised to eat beans, dried peas, spinach, lettuce, raisins, dates, figs, nuts, and all fresh fruits. Herbs considered particularly beneficial are Irish moss, vervain, peppermint, and saxifrage.

Lilly is not particularly flattering about this sign which he describes as 'idle, effeminate, sickly . . . representing a party of no action.' According to him those born under it are of 'a short stature, not very well made; a good large face, pale complexion, the body fleshy or swelling, not very straight, but incurvating, or stooping somewhat with the head.' Their diseases are gout, lameness, boils and ulcers and 'bowel complaints caused by wet feet'! Traditionally, Pisceans are visionary, intuitive, and evasive, and are said to make good actors. They lack decisiveness and staying power. At best they are visionaries, at worst they are drop-outs.

Horatio Nelson (Sun in Libra) met his own death at Trafalgar where he destroyed the French fleet. National Portrait Gallery, London.

Page 178:
May. Page from 'Les très riches heures du Duc de Berry'. Fifteenth-century French manuscript. Musée Condé, Chantilly.

Page 179:
September. Page from 'Les très riches heures du Duc de Berry'. Fifteenth-century French manuscript. Musée Condé, Chantilly.

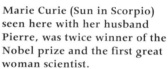

Marie Curie (Sun in Scorpio) seen here with her husband Pierre, was twice winner of the Nobel prize and the first great woman scientist.

Avignon, once the residence of the popes, is one of the cities ruled by Sagittarius.

Nineteenth-century painting of St Petersburg, now Leningrad. Russia is ruled by Aquarius. Bibliothèque Nationale, Paris

They must always beware of alcohol. On the brighter side Pisceans are lovable and loving since Venus exalts in this sign, and Jupiter may obviate some of the less fortunate attributes. Many Pisceans choose to retire from the real world, or are forced out of it into hospitals: the moon in Pisces is said to produce hallucinations which in extreme cases may lead to schizophrenia. Countries ruled by Pisces include Portugal, and towns are Alexandria, Seville, and Tiverton. Famous people born with the Sun in Pisces or Pisces as their ascendant include Chopin, Albert Einstein, George Washington, and John Steinbeck.

The Characteristics of the Planets

Imagine your horoscope as some very ritualized drama: the houses are the stage, the signs of the zodiac are moving scenery, and the planets act the roles. Their exact meanings depend on where they stand on the stage and their relationship with one other: therefore never judge the charac-

teristics of the planets in a vacuum. This would give you no better character reading than the kind found in star columns, which anyway are only interested in the 'meaning' of the Sun in a particular sign. Among factors making planets 'strong' in the birth chart are if they are positioned in the 'angular Houses': one, four, seven, or ten.

The Sun

Man has worshipped this heavenly body as a god since the beginning of time for it is the source of power and light, and astrologers have treated it as a planet from the birth of their craft. The Sun is neither malefic nor benefic, although Indian astrology sees it as harmful perhaps because of its tremendous power.

A well-aspected Sun and Moon indicates a balanced person, but if these are in bad aspect the native will pass through uneasy times with unfortunate relationships. In a woman's horoscope the Sun is linked with the men who will figure in her life, and in a man's it signifies his

career and the sort of life he will make.

The Sun is the male, generative force. It governs the years twenty to thirty, the metabolism, circulation, heart, brain, and sight. Basically, it donates a proud, generous, noble nature, which can lean towards arrogance. It tends towards pomp and high office, and can signify fame or lofty position. If well-aspected the native will be of a noble and generous disposition—a good trustworthy friend. While thoughtful and reserved, such a person is a lover of comfort and things sumptuous. If ill-aspected the native will be troublesome and bossy: petty, talkative, overbearing to inferiors and sycophantic to superiors. As in real life too much Sun can be less than ideal. Too many planets in Leo (the Sun's sign) can make the native domineering.

In traditional magic manuals the influence of the Sun is believed to help in the acquisition of money, friendship, and the support of the powerful. It may also be invoked to find buried treasure. A talisman to attract the sun's influence should be a diamond or a topaz set in gold.

The Moon

While the Hindus believe the Moon rules the intellect Western astrologers claim that it governs health, passion, and emotion. It is female, and connected with water, childhood, digestion, and menstruation. The Moon was formerly much employed in medicine and magic. Manuals recommend its influence for raising the dead, in matters of love, becoming invisible, stealing, and anything to do with travel by water. A talisman should be pearl, crystal or quartz set in silver.

The Moon is friendly with Jupiter, Sun, Venus and Mercury but does not get on with Saturn and Mars. In itself it is neither good nor bad. According to nineteenth-century astrological text books 'if she be impeded of the sun at the time of birth, she leaves a blemish on or near the eyes.' Well-aspected at birth, the Moon gives gentle manners. Its subject will like the arts, be imaginative and fond of travelling. But, if ill-aspected, the native will be lazy 'given up to a drunken, disorderly beggarly life, hating labour, or any kind of business or employment.' The Moon also gives an interest in food, dress, offspring, animals, water, of course, and small items. It can signify home, family and travel.

Mercury

This planet is associated with mind and communication. The Sun and Mercury in good aspect may produce a writer. However it has also been termed 'the chameleon among planets'. It may endow you with a great mind or a crooked one. Mercury rules adolescence, and the nervous and respiratory systems. While giving a versatile nature it may make the native cunning and malicious. It leans towards the middle men in any sort of work and profession, and is connected with travel, materialism, and study. Well-aspected at birth, Mercury will give the native good imagination and memory. Such a person may become an excellent public speaker, with unlimited curiosity and enthusiasm for all kinds of knowledge and travel. If ill-aspected, the native will be a busybody, pretending to knowledge and honesty which have no sub-

Woodrow Wilson (left), the American president who brought the United States into World War I, was born under Capricorn.

'Cymbidium Giganteum' from 'The Orchid Album' (1887). Orchids are said to be ruled by Libra.

'Camellia japonica' is a flower with separate petals and thus ruled by Capricorn.

Franklin D. Roosevelt (Sun in Aquarius), was president of the United States from 1933 to 1945.

Far right:
'The Seven Wonders of the World' showing among other things the various metals associated with the planets. Illustration from 'History of Magic' by Eliphas Lévi.

Mohammed Aly Square, Alexandria. This city is ruled by Pisces.

stance. Mercury gets on with all the planets save Mars. Manuals of magic recommend Mercury's influence should be invoked to obtain knowledge–particularly of the future–and for all matters to do with trade and theft. Its talisman should be an opal or agate set in quicksilver.

Venus

This beautiful planet governs the beginning of adult life and the genito-urinary systems. Naturally a feminine planet, representing sensual love and pleasure, and, while good and kind, it does not necessarily give a strong character. Venus does give attractive, gentle and frivolous natures, and is connected with entertainment and the arts. Well-aspected, it promises pleasure, happiness and good fortune. Badly-aspected, this planet may signify the loneliness of a broken love affair.

Venus in conjunction with the Moon suggests a situation dominated by women– perhaps to do with the sort of job chosen by females. In a man's horoscope such a conjunction might suggest he was over-influenced by women or else had a strong feminine aspect to his nature.

Raphael warns sternly: 'If this planet be weak and afflicted by cross aspects, then the native will be riotous, profligate, abandoned to evil company and lewd women, regardless of reputation or character . . . a frequenter of taverns . . . in principle, a mere atheist, wholly given up to the brutal passions of unbridled and uncultivated nature . . . ' Venus is said to rule those creatures associated with the goddess of love: doves, fauns, and kingfishers. Venus gets on with Jupiter, Mars, Mercury, the Sun, and Moon but not with Saturn. In magic its influence is invoked for all matters of love, sex, pleasure, and friendship. Its talisman is an emerald or turquoise set in copper.

Mars

If Venus stands for sensual love then the masculine Mars represents violence and sexuality. While traditional astrologers could only dub

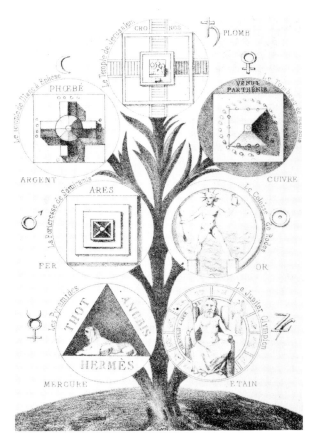

this planet as malefic, modern practitioners have been forced to decide that its influences are necessary to balance those of the other planets. Mars gets on only with Venus, and governs the years forty to fifty, the muscular system, and unbridled behaviour.

Mars gives a masculine, aggressive, and fearless nature, which can become overbearing to the point of tyranny. The sort of events it signifies are conflict, enemies, litigation, accidents, and loss, and also perilous journeys. Well-aspected in a birth chart, this planet gives courage without fear of any danger, an unwillingness to submit to superiors, and the need to overcome enemies while being prudent about private matters. If ill-aspected, the planet will

Luna.

Jupiter.

turn the native into the worst kind of bully or coward, governed by unbridled sexuality. Fortunately for the native the positions of other planets do much to diminish some of Mars' least desirable characteristics. Besides being the sign of military men, the planet is also associated with all those who use sharp instruments and fire in their trades, such as barbers and butchers. In magic Mars is invoked for murder, inspiring hatred, disunity and unhappiness, raising the spirits of those who died violently, and for success in all military operations. Its talisman is any red stone set in iron.

Jupiter

This is the benefic larger-than-life king planet, friendly with all the others except Mars. It rules maturity, the liver, and the bloodstream. On its least generous side it can produce avarice and omission. Jupiter's subjects have a leaning towards their fellows as well as the plant and animal kingdom. They enjoy all kinds of display whether religious or secular, and have an affinity towards banks and restaurants. Jupiter, not unnaturally, is associated with the good things in life: order, comfort, riches, achievement, and recognition.

If well-aspected, this planet gives faith, prudence, a desire to serve, console and guide mankind, justice, honesty, and affection for family and people in general. Ill-aspected, Jupiter brings carelessness, shallow understanding, and little social or religious principle. Such people are easily influenced into rashness and extravagance, have boastful tongues, and are tyrants at home. This planet is also said to rule all 'generous-sized' animals such as elephants. In magic Jupiter is invoked to gain friendship, health, wealth, and invisibility. Its talisman is a sapphire, amethyst or cornelian set in tin.

Saturn

This planet rules old age, the skeleton, and the skin. It is friendly with Jupiter, Sun and Mer-

cury, but at odds with Mars, Venus, and the Moon. Over the ages the planet acquired the reputation of being aged, malefic and very powerful–perhaps because it appeared to be the furthest from Earth.

Saturn is said to give a cautious, introverted nature, inclined to pessimism and reflection. Traditionally associated with laboratories, minerals, places of retreat and learning, it is no wonder that it had a high place in the esteem of Renaissance magicians. The aged figure with its scythe signifies, disappointment, loss, misfortune and celibacy.

According to Raphael Saturn is generally acknowledged to be the most powerful and evil of all the planets. Its plants are those associated

Frédéric François Chopin, the Polish composer, was a Pisces type.

183

Self-portrait of Vincent Van Gogh with mutilated ear. This brilliant but tragic artist was an Aries type. Courtauld Institute, London.

Later astrologers attribute technological inventions to its influence, so it is surprising that they also put themselves under its patronage by being 'the children of Uranus'.

In serious circles this planet's extremely slow cycle is considered to have little effect on individuals, but influences rather generations. Evolving astrological tradition has begun to associate Uranus with rebellion, eccentricity, independence, over-indulgence and cynicism, and it is thought to be antagonistic to marital bliss. Gradually, too, Uranus has become allied with groups specializing in certain skills, as well as industry, capitalism, democracy, fascism and dictatorship—making a host of very weird bedfellows!

Neptune

Neptune seems to govern confusion and exaggeration, which, if we wish to be unkind, would make it the ideal patron planet for some astrologers! It is claimed to give sensitivity, vision and emotional reactions. Those under Neptune's influence may be dedicated to altruistic movements in a rather messy and diffuse manner.

The rule of the seas has been taken away from the Moon and given to Neptune, which is also made responsible for all liquids, including petrol. Because of its slow, fifteen-year cycle its influence on individuals cannot be very significant, but the indefatigable astrologers have provided this planet with good and bad roles. Ill-aspected, Neptune inspires an interest in magic, hypnotism, and an unhealthy wish to 'drop out' from reality, as well as the misuse of drugs. Well-aspected, it influences reformers and idealists. Its influence has also been assigned to such movements as socialism, communism and anarchy, and it has been considered responsible for causing chaos, revolution and scandal!

Pluto

Fresh planets may well be discovered, but until then Pluto is engaging much of the attention of modern astrologers in an attempt to assess its influences, which are still not agreed upon. Certainly, this planet, with its incredibly slow motion, can have even less influence on the individual than the two previous ones.

The latter half of the twentieth century has witnessed a renewal of interest in the occult and Pluto, discovered in its third decade, is now said to rule the unseen, as well as being linked with aggression, the 'diabolical' side of the mind, and Freud's death-wish. Considering the horrors of this century, it is hardly surprising that Pluto is associated with ghastly suffering and disaster, as well as occultism and psychology. Other connections are the Nazi movement, the atomic bomb, spying, secret societies, and sex—in fact, all good headlines for the popular Sunday paper! Optimistic astrologers seem determined to see a message of hope in Pluto's destructive element: that it will lead to regeneration and a fresh start.

with dark, magical practices, such as hellebore, hemlock, nightshade and poppy, and also the churchyard yew.

Well-aspected, Saturn gives the native imagination, reserve, sobriety, constancy to wife and friend, but severity in judgement. Ill-aspected, Saturn produces stubborness, malice, a person always dissatisfied with his lot, and a 'most evil nature'.

Saturn has been much connected with magical practice, and its influence is invoked for all matters dealing with death or injury, raising souls from hell, the acquisition of knowledge, and the erecting of buildings. Its talisman is onyx or sapphire set in lead.

Uranus

In nineteenth-century manuals you will still find this under the names 'Herschel' or 'Georgium Sidus'. Both Raphael and Zadkiel, with noteworthy caution, describes this then new planet as malefic and have few views on its powers.

The curtain must fall on this horoscope play. Should its setting and actors have failed to convince the audience, it is hoped they have at least provided entertainment and substance for thought and discussion.

Saturn. Fifteenth-century relief from the Tempio Malatestiano, Rimini, by Agostino di Duccio.

Acknowledgements

Colour

Aldus Books Ltd, London 39, 135; Bemporad-Marzocco, Florence 35; Benrido Company Ltd, Kyoto 55; Biblioteca Apostolica Vaticana, Rome 34; Biblioteca Marucelliana, Florence 114 top; Bibliothèque Nationale, Paris 19, 79 top; Bodleian Library, Oxford 47 top; British Museum, London 63 bottom, 66–67, 94, 95, 99 top, 102 top, 103 top; California Institute of Technology and Carnegie Institution of Washington Endpapers; Mary Evans Picture Library, London 118, 119 bottom; Photographie Giraudon, Paris 11, 43, 82–83, 110, 111, 174, 175, 178, 179; Hamlyn Group Picture Library 50, 51 top, 54, 58, 62–63 top, 62 bottom, 79 bottom; Hamlyn Group–Eye Graphics 119 top; Hamlyn Group–John R Freeman & Co Ltd 46, 122–123, 126–127; Hamlyn Group–Hawkley Studio Associates 14–15, 106–107, 131; Hamlyn Group–John Webb 142, 143, 146–147, 151; Hirmer Verlag, Munich 27, 30 top; Mansell Collection, London 98 top, 139; Umberto Orlandini, Modena 22, 23, 38, 166, 167, 170, 171; Osterreichische Nationalbibliothek, Vienna 78; Pictorial Press Ltd., London–Anwar Hussein 59; Picturepoint Ltd., London Title page, 70–71, 158–159; Popperfoto, London 163; Scala, Florence 75, 86–87, 90–91; Staatliche Museen zu Berlin 31, 74; Victoria and Albert Museum, London 47 bottom.

Black and white

Aldus Books Ltd, London 32, 45 right, 130 top left, 138, 152; Associated Press Ltd, London 150, 182 top left; Archives Photographiques, Paris 180 top; Bettmann Archive Inc, New York 98 bottom, 109 top; Bibliothèque Nationale, Paris 61 bottom; Bodleian Library, Oxford 82 top; British Museum, London 16 top, 24, 25, 61 top, 80 top, 86 top, 93 top left, 97 top, 100, 101, 105 top, 117, 165 bottom, 168 bottom; Camera Press Ltd., London 176 bottom; J. Allan Cash Ltd., London 182 bottom; Cliché des Musées Nationaux, Paris 69 top; Courtauld Institute Galleries, London 184; Culver Pictures Inc., New York 134; Deutsche Fotothek, Dresden 177 bottom, 181 top; J E Downward 181 bottom; Mary Evans Picture Library, London 14 left, 21 top, 37, 64 bottom, 89 bottom; W. Foulsham & Co. Ltd. 160, 161; Michel Gauquelin, Paris 144 top; Mark Gerson 144 bottom; Photographie Giraudon, Paris 26, 29 bottom, 36; Graphischen Sammlung der Zentral-bibliothek, Zurich 96 top; Hamlyn Group Picture Library 156, 165 top, 168 top, 169, 176 top, 181 centre; Hamlyn Group–Eye Graphics 13 top, 125 bottom, 129 bottom, 140–141; Hamlyn Group–John R Freeman & Co Ltd 21 bottom, 93 top right, 109 bottom left, 109 bottom right, 115 bottom, 122, 128 top left, 128 top right, 129 top, 182 top right; Hamlyn Group–Hawkley Studio Associates 88; Hamlyn Group–John Webb 149 bottom, 153; Henry E Huntington Library and Art Gallery, San Marino 84 left, 84 right; Hirmer Verlag, Munich 33; Larousse, Paris 183 bottom; Mansell Collection, London 10, 16 bottom, 17 top, 29 top, 40 bottom, 41 top, 41 bottom, 42 bottom, 44 bottom, 52 top left, 52 lower left, 53, 73 top, 76 top, 76 bottom, 77 top, 99 bottom, 113 right, 116 bottom right, 120, 121, 125 top; Mansell-Alinan 13 bottom, 40 top, 44 top, 45 left, 73 bottom, 85 top, 85 bottom, 89 top, 92, 93 bottom; Mansell-Anderson 30 bottom, 68 top, 68 bottom, 69 bottom, 80 bottom, 86 bottom, 185; Bildarchiv Foto Matburg 52 right; A Martin, Paris 162 bottom; Foto Mas, Barcelona 72; National Gallery, London 12; National Maritime Museum, London 113 left, 149 top; National Portrait Gallery, London 114 bottom, 116 upper left, 116 bottom left, 130 bottom left, 164, 172 top, 177 top; New York Public Library 77 bottom, 82 bottom, 132–133; Ninna-ji, Kyoto 56, 57 top; Pictorial Press Ltd., London 60 top, 136 top, 136 bottom; Popperfoto, London 18, 60 bottom; Psychic News, London 130 top right; Radio Times Hulton Picture Library, London 28, 57 bottom, 64 top, 65 top, 65 bottom, 73 centre, 80–81 top, 81 bottom, 96 bottom, 97 bottom, 102 bottom, 103 bottom, 105 bottom, 108 top, 112, 128 bottom, 130 bottom right, 137; Roger-Viollet, Paris 48 bottom, 172 bottom, 173, 180 bottom; Ronan Picture Library, Cambridge 17 bottom, 42 top, 104 top, 108 bottom, 116 top, 124, 157, 183 top left, 183 top right; Jean Roubier, Paris 104 bottom; Seattle Art Museum 49; Studio, Florence 162 top; Victorian and Albert Museum, London 20; Victoria and Albert Theatre Museum–J W Debenham 145 top, 145 bottom; William Rockhill Nelson Gallery of Art, Kansas City 51 bottom left, 51 bottom right; Yerkes Observatory, Wisconsin 130 top left.

Bibliography

A. L. Basham, *The Wonder that was India* (London, 1954)

J. Burckhardt, *The Civilization of the Renaissance in Italy* (New York, 1958)

R. Cavendish, *The Black Arts* (London, 1967)

F. Cumont, *Astrology and Religion among the Greeks and Romans* (London, 1960)

R. C. Davison, *Astrology* (New York, 1965)

R. Dawson, *Imperial China* (London, 1972)

M. Edwardes, *Everyday Life in Early India* (London, 1969)

K. Ellis, *Prediction and Prophecy* (London, 1973)

M. Gauquelin, *Astrology and Science* (London, 1970)

R. Gleadow, *The Origin of the Zodiac* (London, 1968)

M. E. Hone, *The Modern Textbook of Astrology* (London, 1965)

R. Jenkyn, *Astrology and Diet* (London, 1972)

C. J. Jung, *The Interpretation of Nature and the Psyche* (Princeton, 1955)

W. Keller, *The Bible as History* (London, 1956)

J. Laver, *Nostradamus* (London, 1973)

A. Leo, *Astrology for All* (London, 1959)

M. Loewe, *Everyday Life in Imperial China* (London, 1968)

L. MacNeice, *Astrology* (London, 1964)

J. Mayo, *Teach yourself Astrology* (London, 1964)

D. and J. Parker, *The Compleat Astrologer* (London, 1971)

E. Russell, *Astrology and Prediction* (London, 1972)

J. Soustelle, *The Daily Life of the Aztecs* (London, 1961)

L de Wohl, *The Stars of War and Peace* (London, 1952)

Index